Hot & Spicy & Meatless 2

Also by Dave DeWitt, Mary Jane Wilan, and Melissa T. Stock

Hot & Spicy & Meatless

Hot & Spicy Chili

Hot & Spicy Latin Dishes

Hot & Spicy Southeast Asian Dishes

Hot & Spicy Caribbean

Hot & Spicy Mexican

Hot & Spicy & Meatless 2

Dave DeWitt
Mary Jane Wilan
Melissa T. Stock

Illustrations by Lois Bergthold

Prima Publishing

Library of Congress Cataloging-in-Publication Data

DeWitt, Dave.
    Hot and spicy & meatless II: over 150 more delicious, fiery, and healthful recipes/ Dave DeWitt.
       p.   cm.
    Includes bibliographical references and index.
    ISBN 0-7615-0543-1
    1. Vegetarian cookery.   2. Spices.   3. Condiments.   I. Title.
TX837.D3897   1996
641.5′6369—dc20   96-29311
                                                   CIP

96 97 98 99 00 AA 10 9 8 7 6 5 4 3 2 1

Printed in the United States of America

How to Order:
Single copies may be ordered from Prima Publishing, P.O. Box 1260BK, Rocklin, CA 95677; telephone (916) 632-4400. Quantity discounts are also available. On your letterhead, include information concerning the intended use of the books and the number of books you wish to purchase.

Visit us online at http://www.primapublishing.com

Contents

Acknowledgments

Special gratitude to Nancy Gerlach and Denice Skrepcinski for developing recipes for this book. And thanks to the following people who helped us on this project: Mark Berlin, Mark Berzins, Giulano Bugialli, Renatto Buhlman, Ellen Burr, Jeff Campbell, Nina Capaccio, Traci Des Jardins, Roger Dikon, Donald Downes, Melody Favish, Connie Galvin, Janet Go, Reed Groban, Jeff Gustie, Sharon Hudgins, Tommy Hudson, Don Jeffus, David Karp, Mary Kinnunen, Darryl Malloy, Mitch Moody, F. Wayne Morris, Yousif and Katie Mukhayer, Rosemary Ann Ogilvie, Philippe Padovani, David Parrish, Mark Preston, Marilou Robinson, Tim Schafer, Frances Smith, Richard Sterling, Jane Super, Richard Walz, Charles Wiley, and Martin Yan.

Introduction

This book is a follow-up to our first non-meat effort, *Hot & Spicy & Meatless*, which has been the bestselling title in the entire Hot & Spicy series. We had quite a few recipes left over after its publication, and we also collected quite a few additional ones.

During the past twenty-plus years of our immersion in the field of chile peppers, we have collected and tested historical recipes, created various dishes, borrowed recipes from our friends, and taken notes on our experiences of cooking with chile peppers. We have also relied on our far-flung correspondents and readers of *Chile Pepper* magazine to provide hot and spicy and meatless creations from around the world.

We should repeat that we are not vegetarians but merely cooks who enjoy a wide variety of foods. As in the first book, our goal was to collect and create hot and spicy recipes in which meat was simply not a factor. Meats and meat products eliminated here include red meats, poultry, fish, shellfish, and all stocks and gravies made from them. We have, however, included dairy products, such as milk, yogurt, and cheese, as ingredients in some of the recipes.

Hot and spicy food lends itself to the absence of meat because of the intense flavors and sensations produced by a number of varieties of chiles. This regimen also works perfectly with low-salt, low-cholesterol, and low-fat diets, so the recipes reflect these health considerations as much as possible without totally sacrificing flavor. Occasionally, we stray from this position, but at least we warn you when we do!

We use varieties of chiles in these recipes, and fortunately, they are more easily obtainable than ever. We do provide mail-order sources, but chiles are also available at hot and spicy retail shops, Asian and Latin markets, and even in many mainstream supermarkets. For those who have forgotten some chile lessons, we have provided a Pepper Primer as an appendix.

A note on the heat scale: We've used the same mild, medium, hot, and extremely hot ratings for the recipes that have been running in *Chile Pepper* magazine for years now. They are based on our own tastes, taking into consideration the type of chile in the recipe, the amount of it used, and its dilution with other ingredients. Cooks who wish to increase or decrease heat levels based on these ratings can easily adjust the amount of chile.

To subscribe to *Chile Pepper* magazine, write to 1227 West Magnolia, Garden Level Suite, Fort Worth, TX 76104, or call (888) SPICY HOT (774-2946).

Key Recipes and Chile Condiments

Our principal key recipe to start the second meatless book is Super-Rich Vegetable Stock (p. 4), which is even more intensely flavored than the version in the first *Hot & Spicy & Meatless*. It forms the basis of a large number of dishes in the book, so cooks are urged to make plenty of it in advance and freeze it. Certain cooks—and you know who you are—will opt for the addition of their chiles of choice to make a spiced-up stock.

These days, every chilehead's pantry must contain fiery versions of basic cooking ingredients. Consider the possibilities of combining Pungent Pepper Oil (p. 6) and its earthy New Mexican chiles with Herbally Heated Vinegar (p. 7) and its overtones of rosemary and ginger to make the ultimate oil and vinegar salad dressing. And, of course, what self-respecting chileheads would serve veggie burgers with ordinary ketchup? They would offer their guests Three-P Ketchup (p. 8), with its pungency produced by a combination of yellow wax hot and habanero chiles.

The famous American satirist Ambrose Bierce wrote that mayonnaise was "one of the sauces which serve the French in place of a state religion," and our Chipotle Mayonnaise with Roasted Garlic (p. 9) is at least good enough to start a small cult. Our final play on transforming normal condiments into hot and spicy delights is Creole Mustard (p. 10), heated up with cayenne and flavored by a bunch of favored spices.

Next are the salsas and sauces. Some people distinguish salsas as uncooked and sauces as cooked, but we don't. In fact, we use the terms interchangeably, because in Mexico *salsa* means any sauce, cooked or uncooked, containing chile or not. Chile de Arbol Salsa (p. 11) is a classic uncooked Mexican sauce using toasted chiles that's great for enchiladas if you can take the heat. A classic Belizean hot sauce featuring the super-hot orange habanero grown there is Santa Familia Monastery Hot Sauce (p. 12). Warning: It is probably the hottest recipe in this book.

But salsas are not limited to the Western Hemisphere. Adzhiga, or Russian Salsa (p. 13), is quite common in eastern Russia, as reported by *Chile Pepper* magazine's contributing editor Sharon Hudgins. This tasty salsa combines tomatoes, red bell peppers, and red jalapeños. Likewise, salsas are not limited by their ingredients, as Cantaloupe-Serrano Salsa (p. 14) and Horseradish-Habanero Garden Salsa (p. 15) prove with their wild combinations. Avocado-Ginger Chipotle Salsa (p. 16) reinforces the point with its smoky, earthy, and pungent overtones.

Three super pasta sauces are next. Habanero-Pineapple Curry Sauce (p. 17) has definite fruity overtones with all the pineapple added, while

Smoked Habanero Tomato Basil Sauce (p. 18) has the smoky flavor of the habaneros or chipotles. Capers, garlic, and basil are the principal seasonings of Caper and Chile Pasta Sauce (p. 19).

Around the world we go with interesting condiments. Thai Pesto (p. 20), from Mark Berlin, can also be used over pasta but is recommended with rice noodles. Richard Sterling, *Chile Pepper* magazine's peripatetic contributing editor, has collected some interesting spice mixtures, Three Bohars (p. 22), which he found in Egypt. Use these mixtures when curry powder is called for.

Two salad dressings and a chutney close out our condiments chapter. Bon Ton Salad Dressing (p. 21) from the famous Bon Ton restaurant in New Orleans is spiced with hot sauce and Creole Mustard, while simple but tasty Hot Jalapeño Salad Dressing (p. 24) will turn any salad into a chilehead's dream. Jalapeño lovers will rejoice at Jalapeño Pepper–Pear Chutney (p. 25), which is quite a different spin on chutneys, combining pears, tomatoes, and onions.

Super-Rich Vegetable Stock

This stock is good enough to serve as a first course consommé in addition to using it as a basis for some of the other recipes in this cookbook. Baking or caramelizing the vegetables before adding the water gives an additional richness to the stock. If you wish, adding a 1-inch to 2-inch piece of kombu seaweed will also add a further depth of flavor. This stock will keep for two days, covered, in the refrigerator. It can also be frozen; divide it into 2-cup or 3-cup freezer containers. The jalapeños are optional for making the stock spicy.

4	onions, not peeled, cut into eighths	1	teaspoon dried marjoram
3	large ribs celery, cut into fourths	½	cup chopped button mushrooms
2	leeks, white part only	½	cup chopped celery leaves
1	head garlic, peeled	1	zucchini, peeled and sliced
4	carrots, cut into 2-inch pieces	3	cups coarsely chopped tomatoes
1½	cups dry white wine	3	jalapeño chiles, seeds and stems removed, chopped (optional)
2	tablespoons high-quality olive oil		
3	green onions, cut into 1-inch pieces	3	quarts cold water
⅓	cup chopped parsley, including the stems	5	whole black peppercorns
¼	cup fresh chopped basil, or 2 tablespoons dried basil		Salt

Heat the oven to 350 degrees. Place the onions, celery, leeks, garlic, and carrots in a shallow pan and pour the wine over the top. Bake uncovered for 1½ hours.

Heat the oil in a large pan, add the caramelized vegetables and the green onions, and sauté for 5 minutes, stirring occasionally. Add the remaining ingredients, except the water, peppercorns, and salt and sauté for 5 minutes, stirring occasionally.

Add the cold water and the peppercorns and bring the mixture to a boil. Lower the heat to a simmer, cover, and cook for 2 hours. Remove the cover and simmer for another 30 minutes. Strain the stock through a fine strainer lined with cheesecloth or a coffee filter and add salt to taste.

Yield: About 10 cups

Heat Scale: Varies

The Chile Pledge

"And everyone knows that chile can also help solve the energy crisis if we can figure out a way to transfer that pungent heat to electrical power. It should be obvious from the fire produced that chile captures far more solar energy in the process of photosynthesis that a good crop of corn or grain sorghum. There seems to be no question that chile is a mystical, a unique, and a valuable crop—and, as we say in our Chile Pledge, we support chile 'in all forms and preparations for reasons gastronomical, for reasons historical, for reasons cultural, and reasons economical.' "

Dr. Gerald W. Thomas, president of
New Mexico State University, 1977.

Pungent Pepper Oil

Use this oil in place of other vegetable oils for a double whammy of peppers, both red and black. When mixed with Herbally Heated Vinegar (p. 7), it makes a dynamite oil and vinegar salad dressing. This recipe requires advance preparation. As a variation, replace the sesame with other oils such as olive, peanut, or almond.

3½ cups corn oil

½ cup sesame oil

8 cloves garlic, peeled and crushed

2 dry red New Mexican chiles, seeds and stems removed, crushed

6 piquin chiles, seeds and stems removed, crushed

1 tablespoon peppercorns

Combine all the ingredients in a saucepan and cook over medium heat, stirring occasionally, for 10 minutes. Remove from the heat and let cool.

Remove the garlic and pour the remaining oil mixture into a sterilized glass jar and cap it. Store in a cool, dark place for two weeks. Strain the oil through a cheesecloth-lined sieve into another sterilized bottle, and it's ready to use.

Yield: 4 cups

Heat Scale: Hot

Herbally Heated Vinegar

For those who enjoy intensely flavored vinegars like we do, here's the one to use in place of those store-bought varieties. Try it over salads, in salad dressings, or in any recipe calling for vinegar.

1   quart white wine vinegar
5   chiltepins or other small, hot chiles, crushed
6   fresh rosemary or oregano sprigs, 3 inches long
3   tablespoons minced fresh ginger

In a large saucepan, heat the vinegar to boiling. Add the remaining ingredients, stir well, and turn off the heat. Allow to cool to room temperature.

Strain the vinegar in a cheesecloth-lined sieve and pour into a quart bottle. Store in a cool, dry place or in the refrigerator.

Yield: 1 quart

Heat Scale: Medium

Note: This recipe requires advance preparation.

Three-P Ketchup

These three P's stand for plum, pear, and peppers—certainly an unusual combination for a ketchup. However, we've seen ketchups made from bananas, so fruity ketchups are catching on. Use this as you would any ketchup—it's especially great on French fries!

2	pounds ripe plums, halved and pitted
5	ripe Anjou or Bartlett pears (about 2½ pounds), peeled and coarsely chopped
1	cup golden raisins
2	yellow wax hot chiles, seeds and stems removed, chopped
1	habanero chile, seeds and stem removed, chopped
½	cup water
1¼	cups sugar
20	whole cloves
3	(2½-inch) sticks cinnamon
¾	teaspoon ground coriander
½	teaspoon salt
¼	teaspoon ground white pepper
¼	cup cider vinegar
¼	cup water

In a large pot, combine the plums, pears, raisins, and chiles with ½ cup water and heat to boiling. Reduce the heat and simmer, covered, until the fruit is soft, about 20 minutes.

Mash the fruit and chiles with the back of a spoon, and add the sugar, cloves, cinnamon, coriander, salt, and pepper. Stir well and simmer, uncovered, stirring frequently, until very thick, about 50 minutes. Remove the cinnamon sticks and reserve.

Remove from the heat and transfer to a food processor. Puree until smooth. Strain if you wish a smoother ketchup. Transfer to a mixing bowl and stir in the cider vinegar and water (as needed for consistency). Pour the ketchup into pint jars and add a cinnamon stick to each jar. The ketchup will keep in the refrigerator for 3 months.

Yield: 4 cups

Heat Scale: Hot

Chipotle Mayonnaise with Roasted Garlic

The smoky flavor of the chipotle adds a spicy dimension to ordinary mayonnaise. Serve this condiment over hard-boiled eggs or on vegetarian sandwiches, or use it as a salad dressing.

1 chipotle chile in adobo sauce, stem removed	2 cups mayonnaise
2 tablespoons freshly squeezed lime juice	2 teaspoons minced roasted garlic
	½ finely minced green onion

In a blender, combine the chipotle and lime juice and puree. Place the puree, the mayonnaise, and the remaining ingredients in a bowl and mix well.

Yield: 2 cups

Heat Scale: Medium

Creole Mustard

Here is mustard as they like it in Louisiana. Use this hot and spicy mustard in potato salads, cheese dishes, vegetable dips, and salad dressings.

2	ounces dry mustard	1	teaspoon dried Greek oregano
1	tablespoon flour	1	teaspoon ground cumin
¼	cup cold water	1	teaspoon dried thyme
3	tablespoons white wine vinegar	1	teaspoon coarsely ground black pepper
1	tablespoon honey		
1	clove garlic, minced	1	teaspoon imported paprika
1	tablespoon cayenne powder		

In a bowl, combine the mustard and flour and mix well. Stir in the water and let sit for 20 minutes. Add the remaining ingredients and mix well.

Yield: ½ cup

Heat Scale: Hot

Appreciating the Pickers

"Chile to me is a composite of all the men, women, and children who have worked in the fields, *los files*. The farm-workers, most of them from Mexico, are the unsung heroes of chile land. It is to them I am always grateful. I once asked Bishop Ricardo Ramirez from Las Cruces what I, as a writer, should be writing about. 'Write about the men who leave Juárez in the darkness at 3 A.M. and come to pick our crops. They work hard all day long for little pay, and then return home to sleep a few hours only to wake up and begin again the cycle.' "

Denise Chávez

Chile de Arbol Salsa

"Toasting dried chiles either on a comal (skillet) or in the oven enhances the flavor of the chile," say *Chile Pepper* magazine food editor Nancy Gerlach. "Traditionally, this is a very hot salsa. The tomatoes tend to cut the heat and the skins can be removed or not. If still too hot, add more tomatoes." Serve the salsa over beans, rice, or potatoes.

15 to 20 chiles de arbol, stems and seeds removed

2 medium tomatoes, roasted, seeds removed

2 cloves garlic, minced

2 tablespoons vinegar

¼ teaspoon ground cumin

¼ teaspoon ground Mexican oregano

Toast the chiles on a dry heavy skillet until they give off an aroma, taking care that they don't burn. Remove and cover with water to rehydrate, about 20 minutes. Drain.

Place the chiles and the remainder of the ingredients in a blender or food processor and puree until smooth. Add water to achieve desired consistency.

Yield: 1½ cups

Heat Scale: Hot

Santa Familia Monastery Hot Sauce

From the Santa Familia Monastery in San Ignacio, Belize, comes a classic habanero sauce. With a little help from Father Richard Walz, you too can make heavenly fire. This mixture can be processed in a water bath if you want to seal it, but it will also keep very well in the refrigerator in a regular ketchup bottle.

4½   cups orange habanero chiles, stems removed, cut in half, seeds left in

1½   cups white vinegar

⅓   medium carrot, thinly sliced

½   onion, sliced

1   clove garlic, minced

2   teaspoons salt

Cover the habaneros in water and boil until softened, about 10 minutes.

In a separate pot, bring the vinegar to a boil and add the carrot, onion, garlic, and salt. Boil for 10 minutes or until the carrot is soft.

Drain the habaneros. Place them and the vinegar mixture in a blender and process until smooth, adding water as necessary to adjust the consistency. Pour into sterilized jars.

Yield: 2 to 2½ cups

Heat Scale: Extremely Hot

Adzhiga (Russian Salsa)

Sharon Hudgins, contributing editor of *Chile Pepper* magazine, lived in Siberia and eastern Russia for more than a year and wrote in the magazine about her experiences. "There are as many recipes for *adzhiga* as there are Russians who make it," she wrote. "I've bought several jars of homemade *adzhiga* at open-air markets in Siberia and the Russian Far East—and each one has been slightly different from the others. The following recipe uses red bell peppers and red jalapeños to reproduce the taste of Russian salsa, but you could use almost any fresh, fleshy, red mild and red hot peppers, in the same volume ratio that the recipe calls for, to produce a tasty *adzhiga*. In Russia, where electric food processors are very scarce, all the ingredients would be put through a meat grinder."

3	red bell peppers, stems and seeds removed, chopped	2	Italian or plum tomatoes, peeled and seeds removed
3	red jalapeño chiles, stems and seeds removed	8	large cloves garlic
		½	teaspoon salt or to taste

Place all the ingredients in a blender or food processor and puree until smooth. Keep refrigerated until ready to use.

Serving suggestion: Use as you would any other fresh salsa. You can also add 1 to 2 tablespoons of *adzhiga* to soups or stews as a flavor enhancer.

Yield: 2 cups

Heat Scale: Hot

Cantaloupe-Serrano Salsa

Here's a refreshing fruit salsa that approaches being a fruit salad. Serve it to accompany eggs or any entree from Chapter 6 or as a dip for chips. Feel free to substitute another muskmellon for the cantaloupe.

½   medium cantaloupe, diced
1   cup crushed pineapple
⅓   cup finely chopped purple onion
3   red serrano or jalapeño chiles, seeds and stems removed, minced

1   tablespoon minced fresh cilantro
1   tablespoon rice vinegar

Combine all ingredients in a bowl, cover, and let sit at room temperature for 1 hour to blend all the flavors.

Yield: About 2½ cups

Heat Scale: Medium

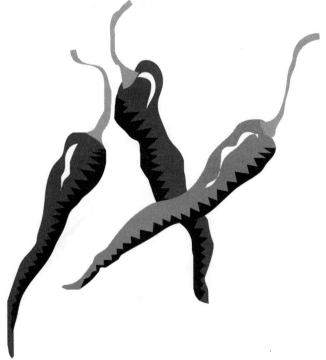

Horseradish-Habanero Garden Salsa

Double your heat and double your fun with this pungent vegetable salsa. Use it in omelets or as a dip with chips. Other vegetables that can be included are mushrooms, broccoli, celery, and jicama.

2 ripe tomatoes, finely chopped
¾ cup finely chopped zucchini
¼ cup finely chopped onion
¼ cup finely chopped carrot
½ cup vegetable juice
1 habanero chile, seeds and stems removed, minced

2 tablespoons prepared horseradish
2 tablespoons chopped cilantro
⅛ teaspoon freshly ground black pepper
⅛ teaspoon salt
⅛ teaspoon sugar

Combine all ingredients in a bowl, mix well, and cover. Refrigerate overnight to combine all the flavors.

Yield: About 2¹/₂ cups

Heat Scale: Hot

Note: This recipe requires advance preparation.

Avocado-Ginger Chipotle Salsa

Ah, another salsa that approaches salad status. Sure you can dip chips in it, but Dave loves to mix it with rice pilaf. He's also been known to make cheese and salsa quesadillas with it. The smoky ginger flavor is quite exotic.

1 onion, minced	1 hour), seeds and stems removed, minced
¼ cup freshly squeezed lime juice	¼ cup minced cilantro
2 tomatoes, peeled, seeded, and diced	2 tablespoons grated fresh ginger
4 ripe avocados, peeled and diced	1 teaspoon minced garlic
2 chipotle chiles, rehydrated (by soaking in hot water for	2 tablespoons olive oil
	Salt to taste

Combine all ingredients in a bowl and mix well. Cover tightly with plastic wrap and let sit for at least 30 minutes to blend the flavors.

Yield: 4 cups

Heat Scale: Medium

A Saucy Christening

New Orleans sizzled when the *American Queen*, the world's largest sternwheeler, was christened with the world's largest bottle of Tabasco sauce. The New Orleans School of Glassworks & Gallery created the 44-inch-tall bottle that weighed 50 pounds empty. It was filled with 21.5 gallons of Tabasco sauce, capped, labeled, and wrapped in plastic in a net to protect bystanders from flying glass. Angel Harvey, wife of the ABC radio commentator Paul Harvey, christened the boat by breaking the bottle on the boat's hull during ceremonies on June 2, 1995, at the Delta's Queen Steamboat Company's wharf in New Orleans.

Habanero-Pineapple Curry Sauce

This recipe is from the Firehouse Bar and Grill in Denver, which specializes in hot and spicy foods. Profiled in *Chile Pepper* magazine, owner Mark Berzins noted: "Serve this sauce hot over any type of rice, potatoes, or pasta."

1	fresh pineapple, cut in cubes, saving as much juice as possible	1	tablespoon kosher salt
2	habanero chiles, stems and seeds removed	2	tablespoons imported Indian or Sri Lankan curry powder
1	onion, chopped	½	cup brown sugar
3	tablespoons minced fresh ginger	1	cup white wine vinegar
1	tablespoon chopped garlic	1	tablespoon crushed red New Mexican chile
2	cups pineapple juice (including the juice from the pineapple)	1	teaspoon ground turmeric

Combine all the ingredients in a blender or food processor and puree until smooth, taking care not to overblend and aerate. You may have to do this in batches. Pour the mixture into a saucepan and bring to a boil, then simmer gently, uncovered, for 10 to 15 minutes until the sauce is fairly thick. Remove from the heat and allow to cool before bottling. Refrigerated, the sauce will keep for approximately 6 weeks.

Yield: 3 to 4 cups

Heat Scale: Extremely Hot

Smoked Habanero Tomato Basil Sauce

Chef Tim Schafer of Cuisine Restaurant in Morristown, New Jersey, developed this recipe for Rob Polishook, president of Chile Today, Hot Tamale, for their smoked habanero chile. If you don't have this chile, try substituting a chipotle. Serve this sauce over pasta.

½   smoked habanero chile, diced
1   tomato, seeds removed, diced
6   fresh basil leaves
¼   teaspoon minced garlic
¼   teaspoon minced shallot

¼   cup white wine
2   cups light cream
    Dash Worcestershire sauce
    Salt and pepper to taste

Sauté the chile, tomato, basil, garlic, and shallot for 30 seconds. Add the wine, increase the heat, and reduce by half, about 15 minutes. Stir in the cream and simmer for 25 minutes or until the sauce is thick. Add the Worcestershire sauce, and salt and pepper to taste.

Yield: 2 servings

Heat Scale: Hot

Caper and Chile Pasta Sauce

This sauce originated in southern Italy. The capers and crushed dried hot red chiles give this sauce body and heat. Serve it over pasta, gnocchi, or polenta.

3	cloves garlic, minced	2	tablespoons capers
2	tablespoons olive oil	1	teaspoon dried basil
3	tomatoes, chopped	½	teaspoon salt
1	tablespoon crushed dried hot red chiles, such as piquins	1	(28-ounce) can crushed tomatoes with puree

Sauté the garlic in olive oil for about 3 minutes over medium heat. Add the tomatoes and red chile and cook another 5 minutes, stirring occasionally. Add the remaining ingredients and reduce the heat. Cover and simmer for 15 minutes. Serve hot.

Yield: About 4 cups

Heat Scale: Medium

Thai Pesto

From Mark Berlin, writing in *Chile Pepper* magazine about Asian markets, comes this Southeast Asian spin on pesto. Mark commented: "Rice noodles are perfect for tossing with this piquant pesto, or use it as a condiment with rice dishes. If you like the taste of garlic, use the higher amount and adjust the heat level with the number of chiles you add."

2 cups chopped fresh Thai basil
  or another type of basil

2 cups chopped fresh cilantro

1 cup chopped fresh
  Italian parsley

1 cup chopped fresh mint leaves

6 to 12 cloves garlic

1 (2-inch) piece lemon grass,
  chopped

2 tablespoons minced ginger

2 tablespoons minced galangal, or
  substitute ginger

  Zest and juice of 2 limes

6 to 12 Thai chiles or any small
  hot green chile

1 cup sesame or peanut oil

Combine all the ingredients in a food processor or blender and process until almost smooth. If needed, add more oil for the desired thickness.

Yield: About 3 cups

Heat Scale: Hot

Bon Ton Salad Dressing

A full-bodied Creole mustard lends a unique, robust taste to this salad dressing from New Orleans' oldest existing Cajun restaurant, the Bon Ton Cafe.

1	egg		1	teaspoon Worcestershire sauce
2	teaspoons Creole Mustard (see recipe, p. 10)		½	teaspoon chopped garlic
2	teaspoons salt		2	teaspoons grated Parmesan cheese
2	teaspoons freshly ground black pepper		1	teaspoon creamy horseradish
1	teaspoon Louisana-style hot sauce, such as Tabasco		1	cup cider vinegar
			1½	cups olive oil

Combine all the ingredients, except the olive oil, in a mixing bowl and whip until thoroughly mixed. Pour the olive oil in slowly while whipping vigorously until all the oil is absorbed. Keep the dressing refrigerated in a tightly capped jar.

Yield: Approximately 3 cups

Heat Scale: Hot

Three Bohars

These spice mixtures were collected in Egypt by Richard Sterling, who was on the trail of the Great Spice Bazaar for *Chile Pepper* magazine. Bohars are used much in the same manner as curry powder, and indeed, they are mixtures of finely ground spices.

Store the bohars in airtight jars and place in a dark cupboard.

Cairene-Style

1   teaspoon ground cinnamon
1   teaspoon ground cloves
1   teaspoon ground nutmeg
1   teaspoon cayenne powder

1   teaspoon ground black pepper
1   pinch ground ginger

Mix all ingredients together in a bowl.

Yield: About 2 tablespoons

Heat Scale: Hot

Kuwaiti-Style

4   teaspoons ground black pepper
1   teaspoon ground hot paprika
1   teaspoon ground coriander
1   teaspoon ground cumin
1   teaspoon ground cinnamon

1   teaspoon ground cloves
1   teaspoon ground nutmeg
1   teaspoon ground ginger
1   teaspoon ground cardamom

Mix all ingredients together in a bowl.

Yield: ¼ cup

Heat Scale: Medium

Bedouin-Style

2   tablespoons ground
    black pepper
1   tablespoon ground coriander
1   tablespoon ground cloves

1   tablespoon ground cumin
1   tablespoon ground cardamom
1   tablespoon ground nutmeg
    Pinch ground cinnamon

Mix all ingredients together in a bowl.

Yield: About ¹/₂ cup

Heat Scale: Mild

Sayings and Riddles

"Many are the cultural links with chile here *en el norte* (northern New Mexico). It crops up in our traditional proverbs, such as the old *dicho: Lo mismo es chile que abuja, toda pica*—It's all the same, chile and the needle, they both sting.

One of our best known *advinanzas*, or traditional riddles, is likewise about chile. *Blanco salí de mi casa/y en el campo enverdecí./Para volver a entrar en mi casa,/de rojo me vestí.* I left my house in white/and turned green in the countryside./ To return to my house,/I got dressed up in red.

Jim Sagel

Hot Jalapeño Salad Dressing

"I think your magazine is super," wrote Frances Smith of Fayetteville, North Carolina, no doubt trying to get in good with our judges of Chile-head Choices. "I can't eat extremely hot peppers but I do enjoy growing a variety of them. I wind up giving them to friends, but I do eat a few, especially in the following recipe."

⅔ cup freshly squeezed lime juice

¼ cup olive oil

¼ cup water

⅓ cup plus 1 tablespoon sugar

½ teaspoon minced garlic

¼ teaspoon salt

½ to ¾ cup finely chopped or thinly sliced jalapeño chiles

Combine all but the jalapeños in a jar. Shake until sugar is dissolved, then add the chiles. Refrigerate 8 hours before using.

Yield: 1 cup

Heat Scale: Hot

Note: This recipe requires advance preparation.

Jalapeño Pepper–Pear Chutney

Marilou Robinson of Portland, Oregon, entered this recipe in the Chilehead Choices department of *Chile Pepper* magazine. She wrote: "A friend's bumper crop of jalapeños made it necessary to find more uses for them. We all like chutney, and since it can be based on almost any fruit or vegetable, I tried using the chiles. It was delicious! We serve it as a sandwich spread, stir it into salad dressings, or as a topping for cream cheese as an appetizer."

 cup minced jalapeño chiles

1 pound ripe pears, peeled, cored, and chopped

1 pound ripe tomatoes, peeled, seeds removed, chopped

1 cup chopped onion

½ cup cider vinegar

½ cup brown sugar

2 teaspoons grated ginger

½ teaspoon dry mustard

1 teaspoon crushed red chile flakes

Place all the ingredients in a saucepan and stir to mix. Bring to a boil, then lower the heat and simmer, stirring frequently, for an hour or until the mixture is very thick. Cool, place in covered containers, and then refrigerate or freeze.

Yield: 3 cups

Heat Scale: Hot

All-Natural Appetizers

Appetizers, also known as hors d'oeuvres, set the tone of the meal. From simple snacks to creative canapés, these bite-size packages of sheer bliss can excite, exhilarate, and entrance.

"Tell me what you eat and I will tell you what you are," said French gastronome Brillat-Savarin. Our appetizers speak volumes of chiles and attitude—sometimes spicy enough to "make your eyes bug out," as our friend chef Eddie Adams is fond of saying. However, other offerings in this chapter are subtle enough to make you feel as though you've experienced a quick kiss of cayenne—a brush of hot with the lingering sensation of seductive spice.

With that in mind, we begin with our first nibbling number, Crostini con Funghi (p. 30). This truly Italian starter is a spread made of mushrooms, garlic, red chile, and white wine.

Our next three appetizers are Middle Eastern in origin. The first two, White Cheese and Tomato "Salad" (p. 31) and Foul (a spicy bean appetizer, p. 32), were both collected by our friend Richard Sterling on some of his many adventures. And who could resist a dish called Babaghanoush (p. 33)? This spread, consisting of eggplant, garlic, tahini, and cayenne, is famous in the Middle East, where many variations of this dish exist. However, we're sure that few are as tasty as our rendition.

Did you know that eggplants got their name because they used to come only in one color—white? Hanging from the plant, an eggplant looked like an egg. Originally grown in India, its purple cousin is the star in our next appetizer, Fiery Ginger Eggplant Dip (p. 34).

Cream cheese dip is always a hit at any party. Our New Mexico Snow (p. 35) is the low-fat adaptation of this favorite, complete with a shot of Tabasco sauce and two jalapeños.

The Chinese call soy beans "the great bean." Throughout much of Asia, the soy bean is a staple in kitchens, produced into tofu (bean curd), tempeh, and soy milk. Our next recipe, Mapo Doufu (Mapo Bean Curd, p. 36), features this new "miracle" food. This appetizer is both high-powered and highly spiced for a great taste.

We admit that our next appetizer will probably not win any low-fat awards. However, we have managed to keep the calories and fat grams as low as possible in the Totopos con Guacamole (p. 37). Feel free to spice up this chip-and-dip combo even more with a bit of habanero.

Want something hot but can't decide what to make? The Bruschetta Southwestern-Style (p. 38) might be your best bet. This chipotle-influenced dip of sorts is great for a whim, as it can be served in soup, on bread, or as a salad dressing.

Turkish food has long been a disappointment to chileheads who love their spice. Happily, our Muhammara, or Turkish Walnut and Red Pepper Paste (p. 39), is a delicious and heated exception to the rule.

The next two dishes in this chapter are pinch hitters; both the Cucumber Serrano Apple Mousse (p. 40) and Five-Cheese Chile Cheesecake (p. 42) are equally at home as an appetizer or main dish. While both are very versatile, the mousse offers a tangy, hot flavor while the chile cheesecake goes down smooth and light.

Have your holidays gotten a little dull? Spice up your grandma's relish dish with our Los Alamos Olives (p. 44). While they are absolutely nuclear in heat level, the taste is worth the scalding risk.

Green onions, also known as chives, are featured in the Dippity-Do Brie and Serrano Chive Fondue (p. 45). This member of the lily family can actually pack a pungent punch of its own, although the serrano doesn't hurt!

Our Mixed Fresh Herbed Mushroom Caps (p. 46) are probably unlike any you've ever eaten. Although mushrooms have been gathered in the wild since ancient times, they were not successfully cultivated until the eighteenth century.

Don't be fooled by the title of our next recipe. While it's certainly fun, the Zippy Zucchini Chipotle Caviar (p. 47) is also worthy of the finest meatless cocktail party—it's hot, zesty, and full of chipotles.

Over the years, garlic has been prescribed for everything from athlete's foot to baldness. Although we can't guarantee you'll sprout a new hairdo after eating our Spicy Hot Gigantic Garlic (p. 48), we do promise your guests will love the flaming flavors of this sizzling spread.

Preparing this dish with the best olive oil you can find will make the difference between the Roasted Red Chile Peppers (p. 49) being good or great. We also suggest a nice white Zinfandel wine and the Green Chile Focaccia Bread from Chapter 8 as the perfect accompaniments to this exotic appetizer.

The last two recipes of this chapter are good examples of simple ingredients turned spectacular. Who would guess a few pumpkin seeds could provide so much magic in our Brilliant Bayou Pumpkin Seed Snack (p. 50)? The Cajun seasonings really spice things up and work as the hot yin to the dip's cream cheese yang. And we finish with one of our most beautiful appetizers, Sizzling Starfruit (p. 51). Presented in a puff pastry package, this sweet yet hot relish of sorts is simply delicious.

Crostini con Funghi

Chile Pepper magazine food editor Nancy Gerlach interviewed Italian food guru Giuliano Bugialli and discovered this fabulous recipe. She wrote: "Crostini is a popular canapé served for the antipasto or appetizer course throughout Tuscany. Pâtés and vegetable combinations such as the following are all popular toppings for pieces of toasted or fried Italian bread or fried polenta."

2	good-sized porcini mushrooms, coarsely chopped	¼	cup dry white wine
3	cloves garlic, chopped	¼	cup chopped fresh parsley (preferably Italian)
1	teaspoon crushed red New Mexican chile	6	slices toasted Italian or French baguette bread
2	tablespoons olive oil		Whole parsley leaves

Sauté the mushrooms, garlic, and chile in the oil for 3 to 5 minutes or until the mushrooms are soft. Add the wine and deglaze the pan. Add the parsley and simmer until the wine has evaporated and the mixture has thickened.

Spread the mushrooms on the toast, garnish with a parsley leaf, and serve.

Yield: 6 pieces

Heat Scale: Mild

White Cheese and Tomato "Salad"

Chile Pepper magazine contributing editor Richard Sterling collected this interesting and tasty appetizer while on assignment in Egypt. According to Richard, the Egyptians call any dish of raw vegetables a "salad," even though we would call this a dip or spread.

8 ounces feta cheese	2 tablespoons minced parsley
2 teaspoons olive oil	1 large tomato, finely diced
2 teaspoons lemon juice	
½ teaspoon red New Mexican chile powder	

Mash the cheese, oil, lemon juice, chile, and parsley together with a fork. Fold in the tomato. Spread the mixture out on a serving plate and serve with pita toast points, crackers, or other crisp bread.

Yield: ½ cup

Heat Scale: Mild

Pod Pourri, Part 1

Chicagoans are feasting these days on jalapeño bagels with salsa cream cheese at one of the many bagel franchises there. . . . A world-record burrito, 3,100 feet long and weighing two tons, raised $10,000 for services for abused children in Anaheim, California. . . . After Gary Waters of Douglasville, Georgia, poured some of his homemade Chef's Boy Hidy Original Triple-X Habanero Sauce on a cigar minnow and trolled it right next to the beach in Panama City, Florida, he hooked and boated a 72-pound wahoo that was more than six feet long. . . .

Foul

Looking for a new and exciting way to spice up beans in a appetizer? Here's Richard Sterling's suggestion for a great starter. Except for bread, beans are the most common and most ancient staple food of Egypt. Egyptians would start with dry beans, but canned ones from the supermarket work well. There are many, many variations; some are main courses and some are snacks, dips, or side dishes. *Foul* is not so much a set of recipes as an approach to fava beans. Feel free to substitute your favorite beans for the favas. We found that black beans also work well.

1	(16-ounce) can fava beans	2	teaspoons red New Mexican chile powder
2	tablespoons olive oil	1	teaspoon fresh dill, minced
1	small onion, chopped	1	baguette, sliced into small pieces, toasted
5	cloves garlic, minced		
2	tablespoons lemon juice or tomato paste		

Mash all ingredients, except the baguette, together in a saucepan. Stir over low heat until it just begins to steam. Spread over the baguette slices and serve warm.

Yield: Party dip for 6

Heat Scale: Mild

Babaghanoush

Here is a famous Middle Eastern dish with variations in every country. It utilizes some of our favorite meatless ingredients to create an elegant first course.

1	large eggplant	¼	teaspoon cumin
4	cloves garlic		Salt to taste
1	cup tahini (sesame paste)	1	tablespoon olive oil
1	tablespoon lemon juice		Green herbs or lemon wedges
½	teaspoon cayenne powder		Pita bread cut into triangles

Pierce the eggplant a few times with a fork to prevent it from bursting. Roast it over hot coals, under the broiler, or in the hottest possible oven until it is charred on the outside and tender inside. When done roasting, cool the eggplant in a paper bag. Once the eggplant is cool, remove and discard the skin. Using a fork or pastry cutter, mash the eggplant flesh with all the other ingredients, except the pita bread. Place in a serving dish, drizzle with olive oil, and garnish with green herbs or lemon wedges. Serve with the pita bread triangles.

Yield: Party dip for 6

Heat Scale: Mild

Fiery Ginger Eggplant Dip

Jane Super of San Francisco, California, says that this is one of her favorite hot and spicy recipes. It is simple to make with a food processor, and the ingredients can be changed to vary the degree of heat. For example, substitute plain sesame oil for the Asian chile pepper oil to "tame" the heat.

1 large purple eggplant	1 tablespoon sesame seeds
2 to 3 garlic cloves	1 tablespoon dried red chile flakes
3 tablespoons dry vermouth	Salt to taste
2 tablespoons soy sauce	Sesame seeds
2 tablespoons chopped ginger	Paprika
2 tablespoons chopped fresh cilantro	Cilantro sprig
1 tablespoon Asian chile pepper oil	

Preheat the oven to 350 degrees.

Poke the eggplant with a sharp knife several times. Bake on a piece of foil for an hour or until the eggplant is very soft. Remove, cool slightly, and then remove the stem and slice into large pieces. Do not peel.

Place the eggplant and the remaining ingredients, except the sesame seeds, paprika, and cilantro sprig, in a food processor or blender and process until smooth.

Garnish with sesame seeds, a sprinkle of paprika, and the cilantro, and serve with sesame crackers, sliced vegetables, and/or pita bread.

Yield: 1½ cups

Heat Scale: Medium

New Mexico Snow

This lovely low-fat recipe was contributed by Don Jeffus. He has been making this cream cheese dip for over forty years and has found it very popular with all who have tried it. Serve as a dip with chips or with a variety of crunchy vegetables fresh from your garden or even as a spread on sandwiches.

2   (8-ounce) packages low-fat cream cheese

1   small jar chopped pimientos, drained

1   large clove garlic, minced

¼   teaspoon red wine vinegar

¼   cup "lite" evaporated milk

½   cup diced purple onion
    Dash Worcestershire sauce

½   teaspoon Louisiana-style Tabasco sauce

2   large pickled jalapeño chiles, stems and seeds removed, minced

Combine all the ingredients and mix with a fork. Do not use a blender or mixer, as the chunkiness adds to the character of the dip. Cover and let the dip sit for 12 hours in the refrigerator to blend the flavors. If it tastes flat, add a little more vinegar.

   This will keep for a week in the refrigerator.

Yield: 2 cups

Heat Scale: Medium

Note: This recipe requires advance preparation.

Mapo Doufu (Mapo Bean Curd)

This tofu (bean curd) dish is spicy, hot, delicious, and unique, and it will stimulate the appetite, according to Mary Kinnunen, who wrote about the Sichuan province in China for *Chile Pepper* magazine. Extra chile pepper oil is often added just before serving. Red chile paste is also called hot bean paste or Sichuan sauce. If the beans in the sauce are whole, be sure to chop them up before using. Serve the Mapo Doufu with white rice.

20 ounces firm tofu, cut in ½-inch cubes

1 teaspoon salt

½ cup vegetable oil

4 teaspoons white cooking wine

3 tablespoons Asian red chile paste

2 tablespoons minced garlic

1 tablespoon red chile powder

1 tablespoon minced ginger

4 teaspoons fermented black beans (omit if not available)

1 cup vegetable broth

2 tablespoons soy sauce

1 teaspoon cornstarch dissolved in 2 tablespoons water

¼ teaspoon freshly ground black pepper

Place the tofu in a large pot, cover with water, and add the salt. Bring to a simmer, but do not boil. Remove with a slotted spoon and set aside.

Heat the oil in a wok or heavy skillet to 375 degrees. Stir in the wine, chile paste, garlic, chile powder, ginger, and fermented black beans and stir-fry until fragrant. Add the broth, tofu, and soy sauce, and simmer for 3 minutes. Stir in the cornstarch paste and heat until the sauce has thickened.

Gently transfer to a bowl, sprinkle with black pepper, and serve.

Yield: 4 as a side dish

Heat Scale: Hot

Totopos con Guacamole

Another tantalizing treat from our friend Nancy Gerlach. *Totopos* or *tostaditas* are crisp, fried triangles of corn tortillas that are served as a scoop for dips. These chips are better if they are made from older tortillas, because the fresh ones are too moist and will absorb a lot of oil and become greasy rather than crisp. The tortilla chips will continue to darken after you remove them from the hot oil, so be sure to remove them from the oil before they are browned or they will end up burned.

6 corn tortillas, cut in eighths
2 teaspoons salt dissolved in ¼ cup water
2 avocados, peeled, halved, and pitted
1 tablespoon lemon or lime juice
¼ cup minced onion
1 small tomato, diced
¼ teaspoon garlic powder
2 serrano chiles, seeds and stems removed, minced
Salt to taste

Brush the tortillas with the salted water and let them sit for a couple of hours to dry out.

Mash the avocados, leaving some chunks. Stir in the juice. Add the onion, tomato, garlic powder, and chiles. Let this mixture sit for 15 minutes, then add salt if needed.

Spray a pan with nonstick cooking spray. Heat the pan on high and fry the tortilla chips until crisp.

To serve, place the guacamole in a bowl, arrange the chips around the outside, and serve the remaining chips on the side.

Yield: 4 servings

Heat Scale: Mild

Note: This recipe requires advance preparation.

Bruschetta Spread Southwestern-Style

This recipe hails from the Georgia household of Nina Capaccio. She says it's a great "make-ahead" dish: versatile, quick and easy to prepare, tasty, and it's even good for us! Serve this Southwest relish as a side dish, sprinkled on a salad, spooned into soup, as a dip, or on toasted bread as you would serve Italian bruschetta.

2   chipotle chiles in adobo sauce

1   (15-ounce) can niblet-style corn, drained

1   (4½-ounce) can chopped New Mexican green chile, or 3 fresh New Mexican green chiles, roasted, peeled, stems and seeds removed, chopped

½   cup diced green bell pepper

½   cup diced red bell pepper

½   cucumber, peeled and diced

1   large tomato, diced

3   green onions, diced

2   cloves garlic, crushed

¼   cup chopped fresh cilantro
     Juice of ½ lime

¼   cup olive oil
     Salt and pepper to taste

Remove the stems from the chipotles and place in a blender or food processor along with the adobo sauce and blend until smooth.

Combine the remaining ingredients, along with 2 tablespoons of the chipotle puree, and let chill for at least 1 hour to thoroughly blend. Store the rest of the chipotle puree in a jar in the refrigerator.

Yield: 2¹/₂ cups

Heat Scale: Hot

Muhammara (Turkish Walnut and Roast Pepper Paste)

There are a fair number of Turkish restaurants in London, according to David Karp, who wrote about the city for *Chile Pepper* magazine, but most of the fare is disappointingly bland for chileheads. The southeastern Turkish region of Gazientap, however, is famous for its spicy food. Claudia Roden, who provided this recipe, says that a tablespoon or two of pomegranate syrup may be substituted for the lemon zest and juice. Serve over pita bread as an appetizer.

1	slice whole wheat bread
3	medium red bell peppers, roasted, peeled, stems and seeds removed
6	ounces toasted walnuts
1	clove garlic, crushed
1	to 2 red jalapeño chiles, stems and seeds removed, minced

Zest and juice of 1 lemon
4 to 6 tablespoons olive oil
1 teaspoon crushed red pepper
1 teaspoon ground cumin (optional)
Salt to taste
1 tablespoon finely chopped fresh parsley

Toast the bread just enough to dry it out.

Put the bread, bell peppers, walnuts, garlic, jalapeños, lemon zest, and lemon juice in a food processor or blender. With the machine running, gradually add just enough of the oil to make a thick paste. Add the crushed red pepper, cumin, and salt. Sprinkle with the parsley and serve.

Yield: 4 servings

Heat Scale: Mild

Cucumber Serrano Apple Mousse

This is a favorite summertime cooldown. While we present it as an appetizer, it is also lovely served as a main-course salad during those long, hot, dog days of summer. This dish is especially nice because you can make it a few days ahead, then unmold it right before you are ready to serve.

½ cup "lite" evaporated skim milk

4 cucumbers, seeded and chopped

½ carrot, chopped

1 serrano chile, stemmed, seeded, and chopped

1 large purple onion, diced

1 tablespoon fresh dill weed, minced

1 cup water

2 envelopes unflavored gelatin

Juice and zest of one lime

⅓ cup low-fat mayonnaise

⅓ cup nonfat sour cream

1 head romaine lettuce

1 serrano chile, seeds and stem removed, cut into rings

1 loaf of French bread, browned and sliced

Place the milk and mixer blades in the refrigerator to chill.

Place the cucumbers, carrot, chile, onion, dill, and water in a medium saucepan. Cover the pan and simmer until the vegetables are tender. Drain the water, reserving ⅓ cup of the liquid. Remove the vegetables and set aside. Return the ⅓ cup of water to the pan, then quickly whisk in the gelatin. Bring the gelatin mixture to a quick boil, then remove from the heat and set aside.

Puree the vegetables in a food processor until they form a smooth paste. Add the lime juice and lime zest, then mix for three or four seconds. Add the mayonnaise and sour cream and process until thoroughly blended. Turn the mixture into a large bowl and chill in the refrigerator.

In a separate bowl, whip the milk with the chilled mixer blades until peaks are formed. Remove the vegetable mixture from the refrigerator and gently fold the whipped milk into the vegetables. Add the gelatin mixture and gently mix until all the ingredients are blended.

Place the mixture in your favorite mold or a round bowl, then cover and refrigerate until it is set, about two hours. To unmold, loosen the edges with a sharp knife, then place the bowl in a larger bowl of hot water for 30 seconds. Invert on a platter. Decorate the edges of the platter with the lettuce and garnish with serrano rings. Serve with the French bread.

Yield: 6 servings

Heat Scale: Medium

Note: This recipe requires advance preparation.

Important Moments in the History of Meatless Dining

- 1123 A.D.: Japan's ex-emperor Shirakawa imposes a strict Buddhist law against killing any living animal.
- December 12, 1778: Antoine Parmentier, a French potato advocate, publishes a paper entitled "Examen Chimique de la Pomme de Terre," in which he extols the potato's nutritional benefits.
- July 7, 1877: Dr. John Harvey Kellogg, going way beyond cereals, publishes a paper entitled "Nuts May Save the World."
- 1905: Upton Sinclair's exposé on the meat industry, *The Jungle*, causes a drop in meat sales, and many people switch to vegetarianism.
- May 11, 1911: The first "all-soy" meal is served by France's Société d'Acclimatation.
- 1948: Campbell Soup Company introduces V-8 Cocktail Vegetable Juice, composed of tomato, carrot, celery, beet, parsley, lettuce, watercress, and spinach juices.

Five-Cheese Chile Cheesecake

This appetizer is both attractive to the eye and tasty for the tummy. Feel free to substitute nonfat cheese for half of the cheeses called for in the recipe. However, don't use all nonfat cheese, since it won't react the same as real cheese or even low-fat cheese when cooked (plus, we'd rather save half the calories and still offer a dish with great taste rather than just a hint of cheese substance).

1½ tablespoons margarine	¼ cup grated sharp cheddar cheese
1 teaspoon New Mexican red chile powder	1 cup low-fat ricotta cheese
¼ cup fine breadcrumbs, lightly toasted	¾ cup chopped green onion
⅓ cup finely grated sharp cheddar cheese	4 eggs
1 red bell pepper, julienned	2 jalapeño chiles, stemmed, seeded and finely chopped
1½ pounds "lite" cream cheese, room temperature	2 tablespoons low-fat milk
½ cup low-fat mozzarella cheese, grated	1 garlic clove, halved

Preheat the oven to 325 degrees. Grease a 9-inch springform pan with the margarine (be sure to cover it completely). In a bowl, mix the red chile powder, breadcrumbs, and ⅓ cup cheddar cheese. Sprinkle the mixture into the springform pan, turning it to coat the pan evenly. Chill the pan in the refrigerator.

In a large mixing bowl, place half of the red bell pepper slices, reserving the rest for later. Combine the remaining ingredients in the bowl. Place the mixture into a food processor and process until smooth. Pour half of the filling into the chilled springform pan. Place the reserved red bell pepper slices on top of the filling, then pour in the rest of the filling. Set the springform pan on a baking sheet and bake for 1½ hours. When the cheesecake is done, turn off the oven and cool the cheesecake in the oven with the door ajar for about 1 hour. Transfer the cheesecake to a rack, remove the sides, and cool to room temperature before serving.

Yield: 12 servings

Heat Scale: Medium

Note: This recipe requires advance preparation.

Veggie Correctness?

"Every day, it seems, there is mounting evidence that eating more vegetables and less meat can take pounds off midsections and add to the life spans of those accustomed to meat-heavy diets. In a 1992 survey, 12.7 million Americans (7 percent of the population) termed themselves vegetarians, and the numbers have surely increased since then. And in the latest version of the Food Guide Pyramid, the USDA has pictured the status of meat in smaller amounts than most of us are used to. There are many who feel the most compelling argument for vegetarianism is the idea that animals should coexist with humankind peacefully and not be exploited for food, clothing, or scientific research."

Irene Chalmers

Los Alamos Olives

This recipe was created in honor of the town that built the first non-food-related nuclear explosion. We guarantee the habanero in these olives will liven up any martini or relish dish with an equally wild taste blast.

3	cups rinsed and drained kalamata olives	½	teaspoon habanero powder
2	garlic cloves, thinly sliced	3	tablespoons balsamic vinegar
1½	teaspoons crumbled dried basil	1½	cups olive oil

In a 24-ounce decorative jar, make a layer of 1 cup of the olives, top it with one-third of the garlic, and sprinkle the mixture with one-third each of the basil, habanero powder, and vinegar. Continue to make layers in the same way until all the ingredients are used, then add the olive oil and seal the jar with a tight-fitting lid. Let the olives stand at room temperature, shaking daily for 2 weeks, then place them in the refrigerator. The olives will keep for 2 months when chilled.

Yield: 3 cups

Heat Scale: Hot

Note: This recipe requires advance preparation.

Sales a' Poppin'

The largest manufacturer of the spicy snack food called jalapeño poppers is Anchor Foods, which is located in dairy-land—namely, Wisconsin. The company will sell one *billion* of them in 1996, according to marketing manager Drew McMillen. "Initially, we had to pay people to try them at trade shows," he said. "But people started saying, 'This isn't bad'— the American palate is becoming more attuned to a better spice profile." Major restaurant chains that feature the poppers on their menus include Applebee's, T. G. I. Fridays, Red Lobster, Olive Garden, and Chi Chi's.

Dippity-Do Brie and Serrano Chive Fondue

This is a great make-ahead dish that we promise sounds a lot more difficult than it is. This is a party appetizer, and the guests will have all of the fun helping themselves.

2	pounds slightly chilled, firm Brie cheese
2	tablespoons all-purpose flour
1	tablespoon margarine
1	serrano chile, seeds and stem removed, minced
1	tablespoon minced garlic
2	tablespoons minced shallots
2	cups fresh pink grapefruit juice Lemon pepper to taste

¼	cup fresh chopped chives
1	teaspoon minced grapefruit peel
1	loaf sourdough, rye, or pumpernickel bread, cut into 1-inch cubes
1	pineapple, cut into chunks
6	green apples, cut into bite-size pieces, sprinkled with lemon juice

Remove the rind from the Brie, then tear the cheese into pieces and place in a large bowl. Coat the cheese pieces with the flour and set aside.

In a heavy medium saucepan, melt the margarine. Add the serrano, garlic, and shallots and sauté until golden brown, about 3 minutes. Add the grapefruit juice and simmer for about 15 minutes or until the liquid is reduced to about 1 cup. Reduce the heat a notch below medium.

Add 5 pieces of the cheese to the saucepan and stir constantly until it melts. Repeat with the remaining cheese, 5 to 6 pieces at a time. Season to taste with the lemon pepper, then stir in the chives and grapefruit peel. Pour the cheese mixture into a fondue pot and serve with skewers of bread and fruit.

Yield: About 4 cups

Heat Scale: Medium

Mixed Fresh Herbed Mushroom Caps

Who isn't happy when a tray of mushroom caps is being passed around at a party? Unfortunately, as we all know, many of those tasty little treats are also card-carrying members of the fat patrol. Happily, we've come up with a mushroom cap that's sure to please anyone who's into taste and watching his or her waistline.

24 very large mushrooms	12 fresh oregano sprigs
3 tablespoons olive oil	6 fresh tarragon sprigs
Fresh grape leaves, enough to line the dish	2 teaspoons cayenne powder
	Fresh rosemary sprigs
⅔ cup minced fresh parsley	Freshly grated Parmesan cheese
8 large garlic cloves, minced	

Cut the stems off of the mushrooms, even with the caps. Slice the stems ⅛-inch thick, then place them in a bowl. Stir in 1 tablespoon of the olive oil into the bowl, and set the stems aside.

Preheat the oven to 425 degrees, and position the rack to the center of the oven. Using the olive oil, oil a 10×15-inch baking dish and line it with the grape leaves. Brush the leaves with the oil and then arrange the mushrooms on top of them, cut side down, so that they are barely touching. Brush the mushrooms with the olive oil. Sprinkle the parsley, garlic, oregano, tarragon, and cayenne over the mushrooms and bake for 15 minutes. Sprinkle the mushroom stems over the mushrooms and bake for another 12 minutes, until the mushrooms are tender but still hold their shape.

Transfer the mushroom mixture to a round platter, garnish with rosemary sprigs, and sprinkle with Parmesan cheese. Serve warm.

Yield: 12 servings

Heat Scale: Hot

Zippy Zucchini Chipotle Caviar

While we may be taking a few liberties calling this a caviar, we think you'll feel rich after you eat it—and you'll still have a few bucks in your pocket and a calorie or two reserved for dessert.

2	pounds tomatoes		2	garlic cloves, minced
3	tablespoons olive oil		1	tablespoon minced fresh basil
2	cups shredded zucchini		½	teaspoon dried fresh oregano
3	chipotle chiles in adobo sauce, chopped		1½	teaspoons Worcestershire sauce
			1	teaspoon grated orange peel
½	cup chopped red bell pepper		2	tablespoons fresh lemon juice
½	cup chopped onion			Pita bread, cut into 15 wedges
¼	cup minced fresh parsley			and toasted

Bring a large pot of water to boil. Place the tomatoes in the water for 20 minutes to blanche. Remove the tomatoes from the water, then peel, seed, and chop them. Set aside.

Heat the oil in a large heavy skillet over medium heat. Place the zucchini, chipotles, bell pepper, onion, parsley, cloves, basil, and oregano in the pan and sauté for about 4 minutes. Stir in the tomatoes, Worcestershire sauce, and orange peel. Refrigerate until well chilled, at least 3 hours.

Right before serving, drain off the excess liquid, add the lemon juice, and toss gently. Transfer to a bowl and serve with the pita bread.

Yield: 3 cups

Heat Scale: Medium

Note: This recipe requires advance preparation.

Spicy Hot Gigantic Garlic

OK, so what we're really talking about here is elephant garlic; gigantic garlic just sounds so, well, BIG! No matter what the size of the garlic in this recipe, we promise a huge hit and more than a taste of heat. This appetizer is easy, fast, and delicious. Who could ask for more?

8	whole heads elephant garlic	4	sprigs fresh rosemary, crumbled
¼	cup margarine		
2	teaspoons New Mexican red chile powder	8	flour tortillas, cut into wedges

Peel the outer skin layers of garlic, leaving the cloves and head intact. Place all of the heads on a double thickness of foil. Place the margarine in a large, nonmetallic coffee cup and microwave it in 15-second increments until it is melted. Remove the butter from the microwave and stir in the chile powder and rosemary. Brush the garlic with the margarine mixture, then fold up the garlic in the foil and seal. Cook the garlic over hot coals, turning occasionally, for about 45 minutes, or bake in a 300 degree oven for 1 hour.

Serve one whole head of garlic per person. Instruct your guests to squeeze the cooked garlic on the top of the tortilla wedges.

Yield: 8 servings

Heat Scale: Medium

Roasted Red Chile Peppers

This recipe was originally of Italian origin, and it called for roasted red bell peppers. We figured that if red bells would be good, red chile would be better! It's best served with your favorite focaccia bread from Chapter 8.

8	large, fresh red New Mexican chiles, cut in half lengthwise, stems and seeds removed	½	cup Italian extra-virgin olive oil Ground black pepper and salt to taste
4	large tomatoes	1	small bunch fresh cilantro
4	cloves garlic, peeled and thinly sliced		

Preheat the oven to 350 degrees. Move the oven rack to the highest shelf. Lay the chiles on a lightly oiled baking sheet, cut side up. Put the tomatoes in a large bowl, and pour boiling water over them. Leave the tomatoes in the water for 1 to 2 minutes, then drain the water and peel the tomatoes, using a cloth to protect your hands. Cut the peeled tomatoes into quarters and place one quarter in each chile half.

Distribute the garlic slices equally among the chile halves, then sprinkle some of the olive oil into each chile and season to taste with pepper and salt. Place the peppers in the oven and roast for 1 hour.

Place the peppers on a platter in a circular design and pour the juices over the top. Garnish with cilantro.

Yield: 4 servings

Heat Scale: Medium

Brilliant Bayou Pumpkin Seed Snack

Neighbors stop by unexpectedly? Don't panic. You can whip up this fun appetizer in less time than it takes to polish off a beer or two. Of course, the trick is to have these ingredients on hand at all times. This is easily accomplished, as pumpkin seeds last practically forever when kept in a cool, dry place in an airtight bag.

1	egg white	1	teaspoon salt
2	teaspoons commercial Cajun seasoning powder of your choice	8	ounces "lite" cream cheese, softened
1	teaspoon safflower oil		Cayenne powder to taste
8	ounces unsalted pumpkin seeds in the shell		

Preheat the oven to 350 degrees. In a medium bowl, whisk together the egg white, Cajun seasoning, and oil. Add the pumpkin seeds and stir to coat. Spread the seeds on a nonstick baking sheet and sprinkle with the salt. Bake the seeds for 15 minutes, stirring every 5 minutes. Remove the seeds from the oven and let sit for 5 minutes. Place them in the refrigerator if you need them to cool down quickly.

   Place the softened brick of cream cheese in a medium mixing bowl. Stir the seeds into the cream cheese and place the mixture into a small, attractive serving dish. Place the dish on a platter and put fancy crackers around the dish. Add more cayenne, depending on how much you like your neighbors!

Yield: 4 servings

Heat Scale: Medium

Sizzling Starfruit

This exotic appetizer is fruity, hot, and hearty at the same time. We hope you won't pass up this recipe just because it calls for some unusual ingredients; both the cardamom seeds and starfruit can be found easily in most specialty grocery stores.

1 tablespoon margarine	3 tablespoons honey
3 starfruit, peeled and cut into ⅛-inch rounds	2 teaspoons New Mexican red chile powder
½ green bell pepper, stemmed and seeded, cut into strips	1 tablespoon crushed cardamom seeds
½ red bell pepper, stemmed and seeded, cut into strips	Salt and pepper to taste
½ yellow bell pepper, stemmed and seeded, cut into strips	2 packages commercial puff pastry rounds
¼ cup Super-Rich Vegetable Stock (p. 4)	

In a medium sauté pan, melt the margarine and then sauté the starfruit slices and bell peppers for 3 to 4 minutes on medium heat. Add the stock, honey, chile powder, and cardamom, stirring gently for another minute, then set aside. Add salt and pepper to taste.

Prepare the puff pastry as directed on the package. Divide the starfruit mixture onto each pastry round and serve.

Yield: 24 appetizers

Heat Scale: Medium

We Can't Wait Until They Play the Lubbock Frijoles in the Meatless Chili Bowl!

Albuquerque, New Mexico, has the dubious distinction of being the only city in the country with a professional sports team whose mascot is a vegetable—or wait a minute, isn't that a fruit? Yes, folks, the New Mexico Chiles soccer team is a full-fledged member of the USISL (United States Interregional Soccer League), along with the Austin Sockadillos, the South Florida Flamingos, the Memphis Jackals, the Des Moines Menace, the Santa Cruz Surf, and the Hawaii Tsunami (we are not making this up).

Fred Matteucci, owner of the Chiles, has bragged that the Chiles cheerleaders chant: "Two, four, six, eight, what do we appreciate? Chiles!"

Organically
Spiced Salads

While health food fads come and go, the longevity of the salad speaks for itself. In fact, an entire discourse was written on salads in 1698 by John Evelyn, who allowed, "By reason of its soporiferous quality, lettuce ever was, and still continues, the principal foundation of the universal tribe of salads, which is to cool and refresh, besides its other properties (which included a beneficial effect on morals, temperance, and chastity)." While we can't guarantee how the salads we've created in this chapter will affect your character, we can promise that things have heated up just a little since Mr. Evelyn was dreaming about lettuce.

Our devilish selections of salads begins with Mark Berlin's Tofu and Cucumber Salad with Spicy Peanut Sauce (p. 57). Tofu is a wonderful addition to any meal, as it is perfect for absorbing rich flavors without all of the fat or calories. The next cucumber recipe, Sichuan Cucumber Salad (p. 58), is not only good, it's good for you with its dual punch of garlic and chile paste. It's a cooling and refreshing salad to serve on hot summer days.

Our next recipe is one of the more unusual in this chapter: La Phet, or Green Tea Salad (p. 59). You may want to make this salad if you feel a cold coming on, as it is full of garlic, whose healing powers are sure to help whip the common cold.

Another exotic recipe (with an incredibly long title) is Kula Greens with Ginger Chile Vinaigrette and Caramelized Macadamia Nuts (p. 60), and the flavor of this salad is unique. Tropical macadamia nuts are readily available in most large grocery stores, specialty stores, and by mail order. A reminder: if you cannot get very fresh farm eggs, make sure you coddle the eggs first to avoid salmonella.

A recipe from the Russian Far East is White Radish Salad (p. 62), which features daikon, a large Japanese radish; the name derives from the Japanese words *dai* (large) and *kon* (root). The spice from the radishes is contrasted with the addition of apples and sour cream. Another recipe with contrasting tastes is Horn of Plenty Salad (p. 63), which has plenty of blue cheese and crunchy walnuts. Once again, apples temper the taste for a fine meld of flavors that blend with the zing of poblano chiles.

Our friend David Karp enjoyed the Sudanese Tomato Salad (p. 64) while on assignment for *Chile Pepper* magazine in London. The recipe is easy yet delicious, and it is best made with the freshest tomatoes available.

Slightly more complicated and with many more ingredients is the Many Vegetables Salad (p. 65). It can be served with any of the entrees from Chapter 6; the many versatile ingredients vary in texture from crunchy to smooth.

The addition of chickpeas (also known as garbanzo beans) adds some protein and a slightly nutty taste to this terrific salad. The crunchy Southwest Coleslaw (p. 66) gets an additional crunch with the addition of jicama. Often called the Mexican potato, jicama has a texture similar to that of the water chestnut. If you're watching your calories, use a good-quality, reduced-fat mayonnaise.

Zucchini Ensalada (p. 67) is a salad to serve especially in the summer, when you can pick the zucchini right from your garden (and breathe a sigh of relief knowing that you have found yet one more recipe for those prolific producers). The multitude of ingredients really enhances the flavor of the salad. You can impress your friends with historical information by telling them that avocados were called "midshipman's butter" by old Spanish sailors.

Another common vegetable, cauliflower, receives gourmet treatment in the Colorful Cauliflower Salad (p. 68). Even though Mark Twain said that the cauliflower is nothing but a cabbage with a college education, cauliflower is one of the crucifers that nutritionists are touting. Ladies, consider this recipe a tasty way to possibly increase your levels of good estrogen; the guys can eat it too—for the vitamin C and iron. Many ingredients are used in the Cinco de Mayo Bean Salad (p. 69), but you probably have most of them in your cupboard already. Several New World foods are combined in this salad: the lima bean (named for Lima, Peru, where it is from) has been used since the 1500s. So, you can tell your friends you're making a really old salad! The heat is from the habanero, which is from the Yucatan and is another New World ingredient.

We would be remiss (and some would say shot) if we didn't include a potato salad or two in this chapter. However, as you might guess, our Pungent Potato Salad with Lime Chipotle Dressing (p. 70) is nowhere near the mustard/mayonnaise version of your childhood. It's smoky and tart—a true picnic treat. It seems ironic that the ancient Incas cultivated the potato for thousands of years, yet now potato salad in the U.S. is practically synonymous with picnics and the Fourth of July. Try the Red, White, and Blue Potato Salad (p. 72), and your taste buds will burst like fireworks. Our next salad, East Meets West Mushroom Butter Lettuce Salad (p. 71), is also eclectic in taste. We've combined the ingredients of pine nuts, butter lettuce, and chile oil to create an unlikely yet delicious combination.

Our next four offerings are fruity in flavor, starting with the involved Chilied Cantaloupe, Cranberry, and Bean Salad (p. 74), then moving to the hearty Hot Habanero Mango Bulgur Salad (p. 76), which is relatively easy to make, but beware of the habaneros—even though we only call for one-quarter of a pod, it still packs a powerful punch. The Peppered Pineapple Fruit Salad with Cayenne Turnips (p. 75) combines citrus with cayenne, along with turnips, melon, and pineapple. It's truly a crunchy, spiced-out spectacular.

Another spectacular fruit-based salad is Key West Salad (p. 78). It is a bit unusual (the salad is laced with tequila and lime), but this salad will rate second helpings. The fresh pineapple adds a refreshing note, while the papaya, called "the fruit of the angels" by Columbus, will help aid digestion because of its papain content (which is always helpful after too much tequila!).

All dressed up and no place to go? Not our salads! We have created a dressing that will bite you back a bit. The Horseradish-Cilantro Tomato Vinaigrette (p. 79) is sure to please and tease.

Tofu and Cucumber Salad with Spicy Peanut Sauce

Mark Berlin collected this recipe while writing about Asian markets in *Chile Pepper* magazine. He created this super spicy salad using a hybrid of Indonesian/Thai satay and Sichuan/Hunan peanut sauces. This recipe transforms mild-mannered tofu and cucumbers into a memorable salad.

Spicy Peanut Sauce:

4   cloves garlic, minced

1   tablespoon sesame oil or sesame chili oil

¼   cup ground red New Mexican chile powder

½   cup mushroom soy or regular soy sauce

½   cup hoisin sauce

¼   cup *sambal badjak* (Indonesian chile paste), or substitute ¼ cup sautéed onions

¼   cup rice vinegar

1   cup dry roasted peanuts, or substitute ⅔ cup chunky peanut butter

Sauté the garlic in the oil until golden. Stir in the chile powder and then stir in the soy sauce, hoisin sauce, *sambal badjak*, vinegar, and peanuts. Bring the mixture to a simmer, then remove it from the heat and let it cool slightly. Using a hand blender, food processor, or standard blender, process the mixture until it is very smooth. Let it cool thoroughly.

Tofu and Cucumber Salad:

1   medium napa cabbage or green or red cabbage or iceberg lettuce, shredded

1   pound block firm tofu, cut in ¾-inch cubes

3   cucumbers, peeled, seeded, and cubed

Divide the cabbage between six salad plates and arrange the tofu and cucumber in an attractive pile on the top. Drizzle the peanut sauce on top and serve immediately.

Yield: 6 servings

Heat Scale: Medium

Sichuan Cucumber Salad

This unusual salad is from Martin Yan, when he was profiled in "Flame and Fortune" in *Chile Pepper* magazine. It is easy to make and easy to eat. The ingredients all meld together to produce a salad that is excellent to serve with almost any dish.

Cucumber Salad:

1   large cucumber
1   teaspoon salt

Cut the cucumber in half lengthwise, then cut each half crosswise into ¼-inch slices. Combine the cucumber slices and salt. Stir to coat and let stand for 30 minutes. Rinse and pat dry with paper towels.

Dressing:

3   tablespoons cooking oil
3   tablespoons minced garlic
1½   teaspoons ground toasted Sichuan peppercorns
2   tablespoons rice vinegar

2   teaspoons sesame oil
2   teaspoons sugar
1   teaspoon Lee Kum Kee Chili Garlic Sauce, or substitute your favorite Asian chile paste

Heat the cooking oil in a saucepan over medium heat. Add the garlic and Sichuan peppercorns; cook until fragrant. Remove to a bowl and let cool. Add the remaining dressing ingredients and mix until well blended. Pour over cucumber slices and mix well. Serve at room temperature or refrigerate and serve cold.

Yield: 4 servings

Heat Scale: Mild

Note: This recipe requires advance preparation.

La Phet (Green Tea Salad)

This recipe was collected by our friend Richard Sterling on his trip to Burma. It was graciously provided by Renatto Buhlman, executive chef of the Strand Hotel. Renatto says to use the best-quality unscented tea available. At the Strand they give you a fork, but everywhere else you eat this with your fingers.

6	cloves garlic, sliced	¼	teaspoon sugar
¼	cup peanut oil	¾	cup finely shredded napa cabbage or bok choy
⅓	cup loose green tea leaves		Juice of ½ lime
2	tablespoons coarsely chopped peanuts	¼	teaspoon cayenne powder
1	tablespoon toasted sesame seeds		Lime wedges
			Whole dried red chiles

Fry the garlic in 2 teaspoons of the oil until it starts to brown.

Combine the tea leaves and the remainder of the oil, and, using your fingers, knead the oil into the leaves until the oil is well distributed. Let the mixture sit at least 1 hour or until the leaves soften. If your tea is extremely dry, you may want to add a few drops of water. Add the garlic, peanuts, sesame seeds, sugar, cabbage, lime juice, and cayenne and mix well. Garnish with lime wedges and chiles and serve.

Serving suggestion: *La Phet* makes an excellent appetizer with chips and a lager beer or a dry sparkling wine. In Hawaii, you might try a Maui Blanc dry pineapple wine. At any rate, don't take it with iced tea!

Yield: 4 servings

Heat Scale: Mild

Note: This recipe requires advance preparation.

Kula Greens with Ginger Chile Vinaigrette and Carmelized Macadamia Nuts

When Melissa attended the Chefs' Festival at the Kapalua Wine Symposium, Roger Dikon (executive chef, Maui Prince Hotel), gave her this exotic and terrific recipe. Serve it at your next party to really impress your guests with your good taste.

Dressing:

3	egg yolks	1	tablespoon Dijon mustard
⅓	cup minced ginger	2	fresh piquin or serrano chiles, stems and seeds removed, diced
2	tablespoons soy sauce (preferably Japanese *shoyu*)		
2	tablespoons rice vinegar	1½	cups macadamia nut oil or peanut oil
1	teaspoon dark sesame oil		
1	teaspoon honey	2	tablespoons water
1	teaspoon salt		Juice of 1 lemon

In a blender or food processor, mix the egg yolks, ginger, and soy sauce for 10 seconds. Add the vinegar, sesame oil, honey, salt, mustard, and chiles and mix well. Blend or pulse at low speed and slowly add the nut oil. As the dressing thickens, slowly add the water and lemon juice. Chill before serving.

Caramelized Macadamia Nuts:

1 tablespoon dark brown sugar

2 tablespoons water

¾ cup diced macadamia nuts

Heat the sugar in a heavy skillet until it melts. Stir in the water, add the nuts, and cook, stirring constantly, until the nuts are sugar-coated and the water has evaporated. Cool to room temperature.

Salad:

1½ cups Kula greens
(mixed baby lettuce)

1 cup dried mixed fruit, such
as papaya, mango, cherries,
or raisins

To assemble the salad: Thoroughly toss the dressing with the greens until well coated. Sprinkle in the dried fruits and garnish with the macadamia nuts.

Yield: 4 servings

Heat Scale: Medium

Note: This recipe requires advance preparation.

El Sueño Picante

"I dream of a green mercado, people in front of their chile stands arranging and polishing the chile until it shines. The air is thick with the healing, medicinal smell of chiles. Everyone, including myself, is delighted to be where we are: among chile. I notice several people to my right. Their faces are totally green, shiny, with that beautiful translucency of chile."

Denise Chávez

White Radish Salad

Sharon Hudgins found this recipe when she was living in the Russian Far East, where it was made with large, white Japanese daikon radishes. The same recipe would be made in European Russia with the large, bulbous white radishes that grow there.

2	large daikon radishes, peeled and shredded	1	apple, peeled, cored, and shredded
1	teaspoon salt	4	to 6 tablespoons sour cream
1	teaspoon sugar		
1	to 2 hard-boiled eggs, peeled and chopped		

Place the daikon in a bowl. Sprinkle the salt and sugar over the top and toss to mix well. Let the radishes sit at room temperature for 30 minutes. Transfer the radishes to a large sieve and press firmly on the shredded pieces to get out as much moisture as possible. Discard the liquid.

Return the daikon to the bowl, toss with a fork to separate the pieces, and add the egg(s) and apple. Stir in the sour cream, mixing gently but thoroughly, and serve.

Yield: 4 servings

Heat Scale: Mild

Note: This recipe requires advance preparation.

Horn of Plenty Salad

The "horn" in this salad is actually a roasted poblano chile. The stuffing is a zesty mixture that is both rich and refreshing, with a contrast of textures. Serve it with one of the less rich main dishes in Chapter 6.

4   poblano chiles, roasted, peeled, seeds removed

2   cups finely diced apples, such as Pippin

1   fresh lemon

1   cup crumbled blue cheese

¾   cup chopped walnuts

4   cups mixed salad greens

⅔   cup extra-virgin olive oil

⅓   cup red wine vinegar

Allow the poblano chiles to reach room temperature before peeling them, being careful to keep the chiles whole and not tear them. Place the chiles on paper towels and refrigerate them.

Place the apples in a ceramic bowl and squeeze just enough lemon juice to lightly coat the apples. This step will prevent the apple from turning brown and keep them attractive, especially if this dish is prepared an hour or two ahead of time.

Combine the cheese and walnuts with the apples and toss. Stuff this mixture into the poblano chiles.

Arrange the stuffed chiles on a bed of the mixed salad greens.

Whisk the olive oil and vinegar together in a small bowl and pour the dressing over the chiles and lettuce. Serve immediately.

Yield: 4 servings

Heat Scale: Mild

Salata Tomatim Bel Daqua (Sudanese Tomato Salad)

If you're lucky, like David Karp, you have friends all over the world who prepare incredible, adventurous meals. David discovered this recipe while exploring hot and spicy London. There, he met Yousif and Katie Mukhayer, who served this at a splendid Sudanese banquet in their home.

5	tomatoes, seeds removed, diced	4	sprigs Italian parsley, finely chopped
4	green onions, finely chopped	½	cup vegetable oil
1	to 2 small green chiles, such as Thai, stems and seeds removed, minced	¼	cup smooth peanut butter
			Juice of 2 limes
			Salt to taste

Combine the tomatoes, green onions, chiles, and parsley in a bowl and set aside.

Whisk the oil into the peanut butter until smooth. Stir in the lime juice and season with salt. If the dressing is too thick, thin it with a tablespoon or two of water.

Gently toss the vegetable mixture with the dressing until lightly coated.

Yield: 6 servings

Heat Scale: Mild

Many Vegetables Salad

This salad has a few basic ingredients, but it is also ripe to receive odds and ends from your refrigerator. If you don't have alfalfa sprouts, for example, substitute bean sprouts. If you have a garden, the freshness of this salad will be further enhanced.

1	head romaine lettuce, washed and torn into pieces
1	cup broccoli florets
½	cup diced jicama or raw turnip
2	scallions, sliced
2	yellow Hungarian wax peppers, seeds and stems removed, cut into rings
5	radishes, sliced
1	cup cooked chickpeas (garbanzo beans)
½	cup alfalfa sprouts
2	tablespoons toasted sesame seeds

1½	cups diced tomatoes
2	pimientos, diced
⅔	cup olive oil
2	tablespoons chile oil
3	tablespoons rice vinegar
1	clove garlic, minced and crushed
½	teaspoon dry mustard
½	teaspoon soy sauce
¼	teaspoon salt
¼	teaspoon freshly ground white pepper

Place the lettuce, broccoli, jicama, scallions, wax peppers, radishes, chickpeas, alfalfa sprouts, sesame seeds, tomatoes, and pimientos in a large salad bowl and lightly toss the mixture.

In a small glass jar, place the olive oil, chile oil, vinegar, garlic, mustard, soy sauce, salt, and pepper and shake thoroughly.

Pour the dressing over the tossed vegetables and toss again lightly. Serve immediately.

Yield: 6 servings

Heat Scale: Mild

Southwest Coleslaw

This refreshing coleslaw complements any main dish. We thank Jeff Campbell of the Stonewall Chili Pepper Company for allowing us to use his recipe. What makes this slaw so special is his Rozelene's Bar-B-Q Baste & Marinade.

6	cups shredded cabbage	1	cup good-quality mayonnaise
1½	cups cubed jicama	2	tablespoons sugar
2	cups julienned bell pepper	1	teaspoon pure sesame oil
2	cups diced onion		
½	cup Rozelene's Bar-B-Q Baste & Marinade, or substitute a spicy barbecue sauce		

Combine the cabbage, jicama, bell pepper, and onion in a large bowl.

In a small bowl, whisk together the Bar-B-Q Baste and Marinade, mayonnaise, sugar, and oil. Pour this mixture over the vegetables and toss until the mixture is well coated.

Refrigerate for 4 to 6 hours or overnight.

Yield: 8 servings

Heat Scale: Mild

Note: This recipe requires advance preparation.

Zucchini Ensalada

Since zucchini is such a prolific producer in home gardens, we felt we had to include at least one recipe to give you a jump on the crop. We suggest serving the zucchini raw, but if you don't like it raw, steam it for a minute or two.

1	pound zucchini	3	tablespoons balsamic vinegar
2	serrano chiles, stems and seeds removed, cut into rings	⅓	cup virgin olive oil
2	garlic cloves, minced	3	tablespoons corn oil
½	teaspoon paprika	4	large shallots, cut into ¼-inch slices
¼	teaspoon freshly ground white pepper	1	large, ripe avocado
¼	teaspoon sugar	3	cups mixed baby salad greens
½	teaspoon salt	10	large pimiento-stuffed green olives, cut in half

Clean the zucchini, cut it into 1-inch-thick slices, and place it in a ceramic bowl with the serrano chiles.

In a small glass jar with a cover, combine the garlic, paprika, pepper, sugar, salt, vinegar, and olive oil and shake thoroughly. Pour enough of the dressing over the zucchini and chiles to coat it, and then toss the mixture. Cover and refrigerate for several hours or overnight. Just before serving, drain off the dressing.

Heat the corn oil in a small sauté pan, add the shallots, and sauté them until they are light brown and toasty, tossing them frequently to avoid burning. Drain them on paper towels.

Peel and slice the avocado.

Place the salad greens on a serving dish and arrange the zucchini, avocado, and olives on top of the greens.

Shake the remaining dressing and pour it over the vegetables. Top the salad with the crisp shallots. Serve immediately.

Yield: 4 servings

Heat Scale: Mild

Note: This recipe requires advance preparation.

Colorful Cauliflower Salad

Raw cauliflower has great salad appeal, and many people prefer to eat it raw rather than cooked. This colorful salad mix, served on a bed of Boston lettuce, would go well with a grilled portobello mushroom entrée or sandwich.

1⅓	cups salad oil		3	cups cauliflower florets
⅔	cup rice vinegar		2	serrano or jalapeño chiles, seeds and stems removed, chopped
2	tablespoons sugar			
½	teaspoon salt		¾	cup pitted ripe olives, sliced
½	teaspoon basil		¾	cup chopped red bell pepper
¼	teaspoon oregano			
1	clove garlic, minced			

Combine the salad oil, vinegar, sugar, salt, basil, oregano, and garlic in a glass jar with a lid. Shake the mixture until the sugar is dissolved, and set aside.

Place the cauliflower and the chiles in a ceramic bowl. Shake the dressing again, pour it over the vegetables, toss lightly, cover, and refrigerate at least 2 hours or overnight.

Before serving, add the olives and bell pepper, and toss the mixture.

Yield: 4 servings

Heat Scale: Mild

Note: This recipe requires advance preparation.

Cinco de Mayo Bean Salad (or Five-Bean Blaster Salad)

If you want to have a blast on May 5th, literally and figuratively, serve this unique salad. It has texture, color, and flavor. The dressing is deceptive—it starts out mild and then goes wild on the tongue. Serve lots of margaritas with this salad!

1 cup sliced young green beans, steamed for 3 minutes	2 tablespoons granulated sugar
1 cup cooked chickpeas (if using canned, drain and rinse)	½ cup red wine vinegar
	½ cup light olive oil
1 cup cooked kidney beans, drained and rinsed	½ teaspoon salt
	½ teaspoon dry mustard
1 cup cooked lima beans	½ teaspoon dried basil
1 cup cooked pinto beans or black beans	1 tablespoon freshly chopped parsley
1 medium onion, sliced into rings	1 teaspoon finely minced habanero chile
3 serrano or jalapeño chiles, seeds and stems removed, cut into rings	

Combine the green beans, chickpeas, kidney beans, lima beans, pinto beans, onion, and chiles in a ceramic bowl. Cover and refrigerate.

In a glass jar with a cover, add the sugar, vinegar, oil, salt, mustard, basil, parsley, and the habanero chile. Shake the mixture until the sugar dissolves, and then allow the dressing to sit at room temperature for 30 minutes.

Shake the dressing again, pour it over the bean mixture, cover, and allow the salad to marinate in the refrigerator for several hours or overnight.

Yield: 6 servings

Heat Scale: Medium

Note: This recipe requires advance preparation.

Pungent Potato Salad with Lime Chipotle Dressing

This salad is filling and light all at the same time. We've kept the calories low and satisfaction level high by including some of our favorite ingredients, including potatoes, mustard, and chipotles.

2 pounds small new potatoes, skins on, washed well	⅓ cup fresh lime juice Zest of 1 lime
2 sprigs fresh mint	⅓ cup olive oil
¼ teaspoon salt	2 teaspoons Dijon-style mustard
2 cloves of garlic	Ground lemon pepper
2 chipotle chiles in adobo sauce, stems removed, chopped	2 tablespoons chopped chives
1 teaspoon coarse salt	1 small bunch cilantro

Fill a large pot ¾ full of water. Place the pot over high heat until the water boils. Add the potatoes, mint, and salt. Reduce the heat and simmer the potatoes for about 20 minutes or until they are tender when poked with a fork.

While the potatoes boil, place the garlic, chipotles, and salt in a mortar and crush until blended. When the mixture resembles the consistency of a paste, remove it to a small bowl and whisk in the lime juice, lime zest, olive oil, mustard, and lemon pepper. Set aside.

Drain the potatoes in a colander and transfer them to a serving bowl. Pour the dressing over the potatoes while they are still hot, making sure that each potato is coated with the dressing. Garnish with the chives and cilantro leaves.

Yield: 4 servings

Heat Scale: Medium

East Meets West Mushroom Butter Lettuce Salad

The idea of shiitake mushrooms and pine nuts (or piñons) may sound a little strange, but it's amazing what wonderful things people can come up with when they are willing to work with what's in the cupboard. However, it does have a bit of a kick, so don't serve it to friends who are faint of heart!

2	tablespoons soy sauce		2	teaspoons sugar
2	tablespoons chile oil		1	head butter lettuce, cleaned
2	Thai or serrano chiles, seeds and stem removed, minced		12	large shiitake mushrooms, cleaned and stemmed
2	tablespoons olive oil		½	cup chopped pine nuts

Preheat the broiler. In a small, nonreactive bowl, whisk together the soy sauce, chile oil, chiles, olive oil, and sugar. Set aside. Divide the lettuce leaves equally among 4 chilled salad plates.

Place the mushrooms stem side down on a broiling rack. Brush the sauce on the mushrooms. Place the rack 4 to 6 inches from the heat and broil until the mushrooms are brown and crusty, about 2 minutes.

Quickly place the mushrooms on top of the butter lettuce and pour any remaining liquid on top of the mushrooms. Sprinkle each plate with the pine nuts and serve.

Yield: 4 servings

Heat Scale: Medium

Red, White, and Blue Potato Salad

If you have never used the "baby" vegetables, here's a great opportunity to experiment with potatoes. They are incredibly delicious and tender, and they look great arranged on a serving plate.

Potato Salad:

¾ pound baby blue or purple potatoes

¾ pound baby red potatoes

¾ pound baby white potatoes

¼ cup olive oil

1 teaspoon salt

½ teaspoon freshly ground white pepper

½ cup red wine vinegar

1 cup diced sweet white onion (preferably Vidalia)

½ cup chopped scallions

1 cup chopped celery

½ cup chopped yellow or red bell peppers

3 tablespoons chopped Italian parsley

3 New Mexican green chiles, roasted, peeled, seeds and stems removed, and chopped, or substitute 4 yellow wax hot chiles

Preheat the oven to 400 degrees.

Clean the potatoes, put them in a large bowl, add the olive oil, and toss to coat the potatoes with the oil. Place the potatoes on a large cookie sheet and sprinkle with the salt and pepper. Spray the potatoes with water. Cover the pan tightly with aluminum foil and roast for 30 to 35 minutes. Test the doneness by piercing a few potatoes with a knife. The potatoes should be firm but not mushy.

Remove the potatoes from the oven, allow them to cool for a few minutes, and then cut them in half and place them in a large ceramic bowl. Toss the potatoes with the vinegar, onion, scallions, celery, bell peppers, parsley, and chiles.

Dressing:

¾ cup red wine vinegar

¼ cup olive oil

½ teaspoon sugar

1 teaspoon savory or basil

Mix together the vinegar, oil, sugar, and savory in a small covered jar and shake. Pour over the potato-vegetable mixture. Toss and serve.

Yield: 8 to 10 servings

Heat Scale: Mild

Pod Pourri, Part 2

Black Mountain Brewing Company of Cave Creek, Arizona announced that sales of their Cave Creek Chili Beer—that serrano-chile-in-a-bottle brew—have reached 240,000 cases a year. . . . A controversial group home for the retarded and autistic in Boston has been ordered to stop "shock" treatments for patients, including "forcing clients to drink jalapeño pepper sauce". . . . According to a survey conducted by the *Columbus Dispatch*, Pepper is the seventh favorite name for a dog, after Max, Lady, Bear, Ginger, Maggie, and Brandy. . . . A new California "infusion drink" features vodka, tomatoes, jalapeños, and horseradish, which are allowed to ferment before pouring. . . .

Chilied Cantaloupe, Cranberry, and Bean Salad

So you're thinking, "Hmm, what an interesting combination of stuff." Actually, this is a gorgeous salad that is both sweet and tart at the same time. Note that this is also a time-saver, as we happily suggest you use one of the best inventions of the '90s—prewashed and chopped salad in a bag.

1	medium cantaloupe, cut in half, seeds removed	2	tablespoons lime juice
1	cup canned black beans, drained and rinsed	2	tablespoons lemon juice
1	cup canned pinto beans, drained and rinsed	2	tablespoons honey
½	cup diced red bell pepper	1	tablespoon safflower oil
1	jalapeño chile, stemmed, seeded, and diced	¼	teaspoon allspice
¼	cup sliced green onions	⅛	teaspoon salt
		1	bag mixed baby salad greens
		1	(8-ounce) can cranberry sauce

Cut each half of the cantaloupe into 4 lengthwise slices. Cut the peel off of each slice. Dice 4 of the cantaloupe slices and place the pieces in a medium bowl. Cut the remaining slices in half again lengthwise, then cover them with plastic wrap and chill. Add the black beans, pinto beans, bell pepper, jalapeño, and green onions to the diced cantaloupe. In a separate small bowl, whisk together the lime juice, lemon juice, honey, safflower oil, allspice, and salt.

Distribute the baby lettuce equally among 4 salad plates. Place a dollop of cranberry sauce in the middle of the lettuce on each plate. Place one slice of cantalope on each plate. Add a scoop of the bean mixture to each salad and sprinkle with the dressing.

Yield: 4 servings

Heat Scale: Medium

Peppered Pineapple Fruit Salad with Cayenne Turnips

When Melissa was a little girl, one of the things she loved to share with her mom was turnips. She didn't eat them with chile then, but she loves to spice them up now!

Dressing:

1	teaspoon grated lemon zest	½	teaspoon cayenne powder
1	tablespoon honey		Dash of salt
1	shallot, minced	3	tablespoons lime juice
⅓	cup rice wine vinegar		

In a medium saucepan, mix the lemon zest, honey, shallot, vinegar, cayenne, and salt. Bring the mixture to a boil, then remove from heat and cool. When the mixture is at room temperature, add the lime juice and set aside.

Salad:

1	pound of turnips, peeled and cut into medium cubes	½	honeydew melon, peeled and seeded, cut into medium cubes
1	cucumber, peeled, seeded, and cut into small cubes	½	medium pineapple, peeled, cored, and cut into cubes
1	(4-ounce) can mandarin oranges, drained	2	tablespoons minced mint

In a large mixing bowl, mix together the turnips, cucumber, oranges, melon, and pineapple. Pour the dressing over the fruits and vegetables and toss gently to coat. Sprinkle the mint on top of the salad. Chill the salad for at least 1 hour.

Yield: 4 servings

Heat Scale: Medium

Note: This recipe requires advance preparation.

Hot Habanero Mango Bulgur Salad

Mango and habanero offer a tantalizing salad combination. As always, be judicious with your use of the world's hottest chile—remember, you can always add more, but it's hard to take away the heat if you add too much.

Dressing:

¾   cup diced papaya

1   tablespoon fresh lime juice

¼   cup sweet rice vinegar

2   tablespoons Pungent Pepper Oil (see recipe, p. 6)

⅛   teaspoon fresh grated ginger

⅛   teaspoon pressed garlic

¼   habanero chile, seeds and stem removed, minced

Put all of the dressing ingredients in a food processor and blend until smooth.

Salad:

1   cup bulgur wheat

1¾ cup boiling water

2   mangos, peeled, seeded,
    and diced

½   cup shredded carrot

½   cup red bell pepper cut
    into strips

½   cup peeled and sliced
    cucumber

½   cup thinly sliced celery

¼   cup thinly sliced green onion

Place the bulgur and boiling water in a microwave-safe casserole dish. Cover the dish with plastic and microwave on high for 5 minutes to hydrate. Remove the bulgur from the microwave and set aside to cool.

In a large bowl, place the mangos, carrot, bell pepper, cucumber, celery, and green onion. Add the cooled-down bulgur to the vegetable bowl, then pour the dressing over the entire mixture. Stir gently to coat and serve immediately.

Yield: 6 servings

Heat Scale: Hot

Ice and Fire

"Compare Dante's terrible vision of Hell, that icy place, with the heavenly state induced by eating chile, the hotter the better. At the moment of greatest pleasure in eating chile, *el colmo*, as the Spaniards would call it, I find myself enveloped by a penetrating heat, a loving warmth, that leads me to believe, at least momentarily, that all is well with the world, or eventually will be."

E. A. "Tony" Mares

Key West Salad

The flavors of Margaritaville and Key West are all combined in this interesting salad, replete with tequila and lime! (If you're a Jimmy Buffet fan, you'll know what we mean; if you've never heard of him, buy the *Margaritaville* CD.) The salad is hot, spicy, and refreshing; serve it with one of the main dishes from Chapter 6.

Salad:

2   cups cubed fresh pineapple
1   small ripe papaya, peeled and diced (about 1 to 1½ cups)
1   cup shredded cabbage
1   habanero chile, seeds and stem removed, minced

¼   cup chopped pistachios, preferably chile-flavored (see mail-order sources), or substitute pecans

Mix the pineapple, papaya, cabbage, chile, and pistachios in a medium bowl. Chill for one hour.

Dressing:

⅓   cup low-fat mayonnaise
⅓   cup low-fat sour cream
2   tablespoons tequila
2   tablespoons freshly squeezed lime juice

¼   teaspoon freshly ground white pepper
¼   teaspoon granulated sugar

Whisk together the mayonnaise, sour cream, tequila, lime juice, white pepper, and sugar until the mixture is well blended. Pour it over the chilled salad and toss lightly. Serve immediately.

Yield: 5 servings

Heat Scale: Medium to Hot, depending on the size and intensity of the habanero chile

Note: This recipe requires advance preparation.

Horseradish-Cilantro Tomato Vinaigrette

Horseradish is often overlooked as a viable hot and spicy ingredient, but anyone who has ever eaten a dish prepared with a healthy helping of horseradish will attest to its hot and potent powers! This recipe is an adaptation of a classic from the Horseradish Information Council.

½ cup fresh roma tomatoes, peeled and seeded	1 tablespoon fresh cilantro, minced
1 tablespoon vinegar	¼ teaspoon black pepper
2 teaspoons prepared horseradish	1 teaspoon Dijon-style mustard
1 teaspoon honey	¼ teaspoon habanero powder
2 tablespoons tomato paste	½ cup olive oil

Combine all of the ingredients except the olive oil in a blender jar. Blend until smooth. While the blender is still running, slowly add the olive oil until the dressing is well combined and thick. Cover and leave at room temperature.

Yield: 1¼ cups

Heat Scale: Medium

Europe Embraces the Love Apple

"Tomatoes grew easily in the Mediterranean climate of Spain and Italy. They were first used for culinary purposes in Seville at least by 1608, probably in a salad along with cucumbers. As culinary historian Rudolf Grewe noted, the earliest known cookbook with tomato recipes was published in Naples in 1692. However, the author identified the recipes as Spanish in origin. Additional recipes were published in Italy and later in Spain during the eighteenth century."

Andrew F. Smith

The Virtuous Tomato

"Tomato cookery was also loosely associated with many social reform efforts under way in America. Tomato recipes frequently appeared in temperance and vegetarian cookbooks, tracts, and newspapers. Vegetarian communities such as the Oneida Community in upstate New York not only adopted the tomato but also went into business canning, preserving, and selling tomato products. Likewise, socialist communities like the North American Phalanx in Monmouth, New Jersey, grew and canned tomatoes during the 1840s and 1850s."

Andrew F. Smith

Super Hot Soups and Stews

This chapter proves that soups and stews can be hearty, tasty, and spicy without any meat at all. Cooks should remember that the consistency of all the recipes in this chapter is easily adjusted by adding or subtracting our Super-Rich Vegetable Stock (p. 4).

We begin with two Italian-style soups. Chilied Lentil and Spaghetti Soup (p. 84) utilizes the tasty poblano chile for mild heat, but it can be spiced up further with habanero powder. Famed Italian chef Giuliano Bugialli provided the next recipe, Minestra di Pepperoni (p. 85), during his interview with Nancy Gerlach in *Chile Pepper* magazine.

A bisque is a thick, pureed soup, and we have two spicy ones here. Gingered Green Chile Vegetable Bisque (p. 86) combines New Mexican green chile and ginger for a unique taste treat, while Sun-Dried Tomato Bisque (p. 88), with New Mexican red chile, is simply one of the best tomato soups we have ever tasted. Thanks go to chef Norm Taylor for sharing his recipe with us.

Two other tomato-based soups are Spicy Tomato-Basil Soup with Cayenne Croutons (p. 90), which is heavy on the basil and is spiced with chiltepins or piquins, and Tomato and Red Jalapeño Soup with Quinoa and Thai Pesto (p. 87), which combines east and west with its Asian pesto and South American quinoa.

The word "hot" in the title of this chapter not withstanding, we offer the following cold soups that have their own share of chile heat. Spicy-Cool Zucchini and Cucumber Soup (p. 92) is low-fat, low-calorie, and spiced up with green jalapeños. The mature, red jalapeños are used in Andalusian Gazpacho with Red Jalapeño (p. 93), which is our version of a classic Spanish cold soup. We've replaced the fat with New Mexican green chile and habanero powder in our Low-Fat High-Chile Vichyssoise (p. 94).

The next batch of soups takes us around the world. Peppery and Smoky Peanut Soup (p. 95) is from the Deep South, but we've taken the liberty of replacing the usual cayenne with chipotle chiles to give it a smoky flavor. However, cayenne is used in Red Sea Soup with Cayenne (p. 96), which has the flavors of the Middle East combined with chickpeas and basmati rice. From the Caribbean comes Yellow Pepper Soup with Orange Habaneros (p. 97), and Mexico is represented by Nancy Gerlach's Sopa de Tortilla (p. 98).

We love mushrooms in any form, and they are great meat substitutes. Three-Mushroom, Two-Chile Soup (p. 100) features shiitake, enoki, and white mushrooms, plus New Mexican green and red chile; leeks and potatoes give it additional heartiness. Another hearty soup is Mushroom and Barley Soup with Hot Paprika (p. 102), which depends on imported Hungarian hot paprika for its heat level.

Three Southwest-style stews reveal the versatility of the genre in that region. North of the Border Vegetable Chowder (p. 104) is an unusual spin on Southwestern flavors, while Chipotle Black Bean Stew with Pumpkin (p. 101) is Mary Jane's version of a low-fat but classic stew. Some cooks may not believe that a split pea soup can be made without ham, but our Split Pea–Poblano Stew (p. 106) proves that such a creation need not lack flavor. The poblano chiles more than make up for the lack of any meat.

Our final two stews are rather eclectic. White Bean Stew with Spicy Olivada Sauce (p. 108) depends on pureed black olives for intense flavor (in addition to the green chile and chiltepin powder). Highly unusual is Indian-Style Lentil and Chile Stew (p. 107), with its combination of red chile, lentils, and coconut.

Chilied Lentil and Spaghetti Soup

This is our variation on a traditional soup from Apulia, an olive oil production center in Italy. Some of our Red Chile Croutons (p. 219) would be perfect to float in this soup. For extra heat, add some chiltepin or habanero powder to taste.

1¼	cups dried lentils, cleaned and rinsed	8	cups Super-Rich Vegetable Stock (see recipe, p. 4)
1	onion, diced	4	ounces spaghetti, broken into 2-inch lengths
1	carrot, diced		Salt and pepper
2	ribs celery, diced	6	tablespoons extra-virgin olive oil
1	clove garlic, minced		
1½	cups coarsely chopped tomatoes in puree		
2	poblano chiles, roasted, peeled, seeds and stems removed, chopped		

In a large pot, combine the lentils, onion, carrot, celery, garlic, tomatoes, chiles, and stock and bring to a boil. Cover, reduce the heat, and simmer until the lentils are tender, about 1 hour. Add the spaghetti, partially cover, and simmer until the spaghetti is tender, about 12 minutes. Add salt and pepper to taste.

To serve, ladle into warm bowls and drizzle each bowl of soup with 1 tablespoon of olive oil.

Yield: 6 servings

Heat Scale: Mild

Minestra de Pepperoni

This recipe was provided by Italian chef Giuliano Bugialli, who was interviewed by Nancy Gerlach in *Chile Pepper* magazine. She wrote: "This colorful, creamy soup is a welcome accompaniment to any meal, or with the addition of a crisp salad and hearty Italian bread, a meal in itself."

1 small onion, chopped

4 cloves garlic, minced

2 tablespoons extra-virgin olive oil

2 tablespoons capers

½ teaspoon dried crushed red chile, such as New Mexican or piquin

1½ pounds yellow bell peppers, stems and seeds removed, coarsely chopped

¼ teaspoon dried thyme

2 cups Super-Rich Vegetable Stock (see recipe, p. 4)

Salt to taste

1 cup grated Parmesan cheese

Sauté the onion and garlic in the oil for 5 minutes. Add most of the capers and chile and continue to cook for 3 minutes. Add the bell peppers and sauté for an additional 10 minutes. Stir in the thyme and stock. Bring to a boil, reduce the heat, cover, and simmer for 30 minutes or until the peppers are soft. Place the soup in a blender or food processor and puree until smooth. Add salt to taste.

To serve, garnish with remaining capers and sprinkle some of the cheese on top, offering additional cheese on the side.

Yield: 4 servings

Heat Scale: Mild

Gingered Green Chile Vegetable Bisque

The complexity of vegetable flavors in this thick green soup is intensified by the addition of the ginger. Since the chiles are eventually pureed, there is no need to roast and peel them. For a hotter bisque, replace half of the New Mexican chiles with jalapeños.

1	cup chopped fresh New Mexican chile	7	cups Super-Rich Vegetable Stock (see recipe, p. 4)
1	cup chopped celery	4	cups chopped fresh green beans
1	cup diced potatoes		
1	small zucchini, chopped	¼	cup chopped fresh parsley
⅓	cup basmati rice	1	(3-inch) piece ginger root
⅛	teaspoon white pepper		Salt and pepper
1	bay leaf		Chopped cilantro
	Pinch dried thyme		Chopped chives
	Pinch dried basil		Chopped tomato

In a large pot, combine the chile, celery, potatoes, zucchini, rice, pepper, bay leaf, thyme, basil, and stock. Bring to a boil, lower the heat, and simmer, uncovered, until the potatoes are tender, about 15 minutes. Add the beans and simmer until tender, about 10 minutes. Remove the bay leaf and add the parsley.

Remove from the heat and puree the soup in batches in a blender or food processor until smooth, adding more stock if necessary. Return the soup to the pot. Peel the ginger, grate, and press out the juice into the soup. If the ginger is dry and doesn't have much juice, add the grated ginger to the soup. Stir and heat for 1 minute and add the salt and pepper to taste.

Serve garnished with cilantro, chives, and tomato.

Yield: 6 servings

Heat Scale: Medium

Tomato and Red Jalapeño Soup with Quinoa and Thai Pesto

Talk about a multicultural soup experience! We have South American quinoa flavored with a Southeast Asian pesto. The quinoa adds a nice texture and crunch. Serve the soup hot with a generous dollop of Thai Pesto floating in the middle of it.

⅓ cup quinoa grain, rinsed for 2 minutes

⅔ cup water

⅛ teaspoon salt

1 (28-ounce) can tomato puree

3 red jalapeños, seeds and stems removed, halved

2 tablespoons extra-virgin olive oil

1½ cups chopped onions

2 cloves garlic, minced

½ teaspoon freshly ground black pepper

¼ teaspoon sugar

2 cups Super-Rich Vegetable Stock (see recipe, p. 4)

½ cup Thai Pesto (see recipe, p. 20)

In a small saucepan, combine the quinoa, water, and salt and bring to a boil. Reduce the heat to low, cover, and simmer for 15 to 20 minutes, or until all the water is absorbed. Remove from the heat and reserve.

In a food processor, combine the tomato puree and the jalapeños and puree. Reserve.

Heat the olive oil in a pot and sauté the onions and garlic together for 7 to 8 minutes. Add the black pepper, sugar, the reserved puree, and the vegetable stock. Simmer, uncovered, for 20 minutes, then add the quinoa and simmer for 10 more minutes.

Serve the soup in bowls topped with a tablespoon or more of the Thai Pesto.

Yield: 6 servings

Heat Scale: Medium

Sun-Dried Tomato Bisque

Dave and Mary Jane tasted this bisque at Scalo restaurant in Albuquerque, New Mexico and immediately asked to meet the chef. He turned out to be Norm Taylor, who was a visiting chef for only a few weeks. He gladly consented to share his recipe with us. To make tomato concassée, place the tomatoes in boiling water for a few seconds to loosen the skins, then peel, cut in half, seed, and squeeze out the juice. Then dice them as finely as possible.

8	cups sun-dried tomatoes	1	lemon, cut into ½-inch slices
1	dried red New Mexican chile, seeds and stem removed, left whole	4	teaspoons olive oil
		1	medium red onion, diced
2	(5-inch) sprigs young sage	3	cloves garlic, minced
2	(6-inch) sprigs rosemary	½	cup red wine
1	small bunch thyme	½	cup balsamic vinegar
1	small bunch Italian parsley	2	cups tomato concassée

Add the sun-dried tomatoes and the chile to a large pot and cover with water. Turn the heat to medium. In a piece of cheesecloth, wrap the sage, rosemary, thyme, parsley, and lemon slices together and tie to make a bouquet garni. Add it to the water. Cover, reduce the heat, and simmer for 2 hours, adding water if necessary.

Heat the oil in a skillet and sauté the onion until soft and translucent. Add the garlic and lightly sauté. Reserve.

In a small saucepan, boil together the red wine and balsamic vinegar until it is reduced to ⅛ cup. Reserve.

When the sun-dried tomato mixture is done, remove the bouquet garni, the chile, and the lemon slices. Add the reserved onion-garlic mixture, the reduced wine-vinegar, and the tomato concassée. Simmer, uncovered, for 10 minutes.

Remove from the heat and puree in a blender or food processor until smooth, then strain.

Serving suggestions: To serve the bisque hot, add a dollop of sweet butter and swirl across the surface. To serve cold, top with a dollop of citrus crème fraîche or whipped cream.

Yield: 6 servings

Heat Scale: Mild

"Goblin" the Chile

"Even when I am at my troglodytic and misanthropic worst, isolated and wanting no human company, a bowl of steamy hot green chile or red chile—no, I did not say chile *stew*, I said a bowl of *chile*—will bring me back to a psychological condition of identification with my fellow human beings. At that moment, *tengo duende*, I have *duende*. The sprite of good will and creativity is whirling all around me and inside me."

E. A. "Tony" Mares

Spicy Tomato-Basil Soup with Cayenne Croutons

Here's Nancy Gerlach's spin on tomato soup. She commented: "Any small, hot dried chiles will be good in this recipe, even those little ones you've grown and can't identify. If you can't find a thin baguette for the croutons, make them from large cubes of bread. Float the croutons on the soup just before serving."

Cayenne Croutons:

2   tablespoons margarine
2   tablespoons olive oil
1   tablespoon minced fresh parsley
½   teaspoon powdered garlic

½   teaspoon cayenne powder
1   French baguette, cut in ¼-inch-thick rounds

Melt the margarine and add all the remaining ingredients except the bread. Spread the mixture on the bread and bake at 300 degrees until toasted, about 5 minutes per side.

If using diced bread, toss in the mixture and bake, turning occasionally.

Soup:

8   large tomatoes (about 3 pounds), peeled, seeds removed, chopped
1   onion, chopped
1   rib celery, including the leaves, chopped
1   to 2 tablespoons olive oil
4   small hot whole dried chiles, such as chiltepins or piquins

2   teaspoons margarine
2   teaspoons all-purpose flour
1½ to 2 cups Super-Rich Vegetable Stock (see recipe, p. 4)
1   teaspoon sugar
    Salt and freshly ground black pepper
10 fresh basil leaves, plus chopped for garnish

Sauté the tomatoes, onion, and celery in the oil until soft. Cover and simmer for 20 to 25 minutes until very tender. Place the tomato mixture and the chiles in a blender or food processor and puree until smooth. Strain for a smooth soup.

Melt the margarine and stir in the flour to make a roux. Cook the roux for a couple of minutes. Whisk in the stock, raise the heat, stirring until boiling. Reduce the heat, add the tomato mixture, and simmer until cooked to desired thickness. Season with the sugar and salt and pepper to taste.

Float the croutons on the soup before serving, and garnish with basil leaves.

Yield: 4 to 6 servings

Heat Scale: Mild

Pod Pourri, Part 3

A remedy for bruises in *The Healing Herbs* by Michael Castleman calls for mixing one-half teaspoon of cayenne powder with one cup of warm vegetable oil and rubbing the hot oil onto the bruise several times a day. . . . A 1994 Red Savina Habanero from GNS Spices has tested an astonishing 577,000 Scoville Units and is believed to be the hottest pepper ever tested. . . . With the headline "Only Mother Nature Packs More Power Into Such a Small Package," NEC uses a photo of an habanero to tout its new Versa Notebook Computer. . . . Heinz now has a new Heinz Hot Ketchup, made with McIlhenny Company's Tabasco Pepper Sauce, which is being test-marketed in appropriate cities: New Orleans, San Antonio, and Dallas. . . .

Spicy-Cool Zucchini and Cucumber Soup

In the summertime, we just love cold soups, especially when they're low-fat, low-calorie, and spiced with chiles and fresh dill. Why, it sounds like we're describing the following soup, which comes right from the garden.

¼ cup olive oil

2 medium onions, diced

2 pounds zucchini, coarsely chopped

2 cucumbers, seeded, skins left on, chopped

2 jalapeño chiles, seeds and stems removed, chopped fine

3 cups Super-Rich Vegetable Stock (see recipe, p. 4)

2 teaspoons freshly squeezed lemon juice

¼ cup chopped fresh dill

Fresh dill

Diced tomatoes

Heat the olive oil in a skillet and sauté the onions until they are soft, about 10 minutes. Add the zucchini, cucumbers, and jalapeños and cook over medium heat for 10 more minutes, stirring occasionally.

Add the stock and lemon juice and cook, uncovered, for 20 minutes over medium heat. Remove from the heat and add the chopped fresh dill.

Let cool, then puree in a blender in batches until smooth. Refrigerate until chilled, then serve garnished with dill and tomatoes.

Yield: 6 servings

Heat Scale: Medium

Note: This recipe requires advance preparation.

Andulusian Gazpacho with Red Jalapeño

Here's a cold soup that sparkles with spicy heat and flavor. It is originally from Córdoba, Spain, where it is served bland, but we have taken the liberty to spice it up a bit. It is interesting because it is made without cooking and without water.

¼ pound white bread, 2 days old, crusts removed (about ½ pound before crusts are removed)

¾ cup cold water

2 pounds ripe tomatoes, peeled and seeded

2 red jalapeño chiles, seeds and stems removed

1 teaspoon minced garlic

2 egg yolks

1½ tablespoons red wine vinegar

½ teaspoon salt

¼ teaspoon white pepper

⅓ cup extra-virgin olive oil
   Chopped hard-boiled eggs
   Minced cilantro

In a bowl, soak the bread in the cold water for a minute or two. With your hands, squeeze the excess water from the bread and place the bread in a food processor. Add the tomatoes, chiles, and garlic and puree. While pureeing, add the egg yolks, vinegar, salt, and pepper. Continue pureeing and slowly add the olive oil until the mixture is smooth.

Transfer to a bowl and refrigerate for 4 hours. Serve in chilled bowls garnished with the eggs and cilantro.

Yield: 4 to 6 servings

Heat Scale: Mild

Note: This recipe requires advance preparation.

Low-Fat High-Chile Vichyssoise

Of course, this version of the famous soup will be different from the heavily laden butter and cream recipes of the past. For one, it will have a lot more heat for a cold soup, because we've replaced the fat with chile.

2	tablespoons olive oil	1	cup chopped fresh New Mexican green chile
2	cups chopped leeks		
2	cups chopped onions	1	cup evaporated skim milk
6	cups Super-Rich Vegetable Stock (see recipe, p. 4)	1	cup nonfat sour cream
		1	cup skim milk
½	teaspoon habanero powder	1	teaspoon white pepper
¼	cup chopped fresh basil		Freshly minced chives
5	pounds white potatoes, peeled and diced		New Mexican red chile powder

In a large soup pot, heat the olive oil and sauté the leeks and onions until soft, about 10 minutes. Add the stock, habanero powder, basil, potatoes, and green chile and bring to a boil. Reduce the heat and simmer until the potatoes are tender, about 20 minutes.

Remove from the heat and puree in batches in a food processor until the mixture is a very smooth, thin paste. Transfer to a bowl and add the evaporated milk, sour cream, milk, and white pepper. Mix well, taste for heat, and add hot chile powder if too mild. Cover and refrigerate for at least 5 hours. Serve in cold bowls garnished with chives and a sprinkling of red chile powder.

Yield: 8 servings

Heat Scale: Mild to Medium

Note: This recipe requires advance preparation.

Peppery and Smoky Peanut Soup

The combination of peanuts and chiles is quite common in Africa and in the American South, where this recipe originated. Cayenne was the chile of choice in the original, but we've decided to expand the taste dimension to smoky—hence the chipotle chile. We dare you to serve this peanut soup with jelly sandwiches.

2	tablespoons olive oil	½	cup smooth peanut butter
5	green onions, sliced thinly, tops included	2	chipotle chiles in adobo sauce, minced
1	rib celery, minced	1½	teaspoons lemon juice
3	tablespoons flour		Salt
1⅔	cups Super-Rich Vegetable Stock (see recipe, p. 4)	¼	cup chopped roasted peanuts
2	cups milk	2	tablespoons minced chives

In a large pot, heat the olive oil and add the green onions and celery. Sauté until soft, about 10 minutes. Blend in the flour and stir well to make a kind of roux. Add the stock and milk, then heat, stirring well, until thickened, about 15 minutes.

Strain the soup, then return the liquid to the pan. Puree the onions and celery in a food processor. Mix the puree into the soup.

Turn the heat to low and add the peanut butter and beat until well blended. Add the chiles and lemon juice and simmer, uncovered, for 15 minutes, stirring occasionally. Add salt to taste.

Serve garnished with the peanuts and chives.

Yield: 6 servings

Heat Scale: Medium

Red Sea Soup with Cayenne

The flavors of the Middle East are infused into this soup, including a heavy dose of chiles. It is not commonly known that the region is renowned for its consumption of Louisiana-style, cayenne-based sauces.

2 cloves garlic, unpeeled	1 large onion, chopped
1 teaspoon coriander seeds	½ cup basmati rice
1 teaspoon cumin seeds	1 lemon
½ teaspoon crushed cayenne or other hot red chile	1 (8-ounce) can chickpeas (garbanzo beans), drained and rinsed
¼ teaspoon turmeric	Freshly ground black pepper
1 cinnamon stick	Fresh mint leaves
6 cups Super-Rich Vegetable Stock (see recipe, p. 4)	Lemon slices
1 tablespoon olive oil	Bottled Louisiana-style hot sauce

Crush the garlic clove with the back of a spoon, but do not peel. In a mortar, coarsely crush the coriander and cumin seeds. In a bowl, combine the garlic, coriander, cumin, chile, and turmeric and mix well. Transfer to a double layer of cheesecloth or a tea infuser and tie or close.

In a large saucepan, combine the spice mixture, cinnamon stick, and stock. Boil, uncovered, until reduced to 4 cups, about 20 minutes or so. Remove from the heat.

Heat the olive oil in a large pot over medium heat. Add the onion and sauté for 5 minutes. And the rice and sauté for an additional minute. Add the stock with the spice mixture and cinnamon and stir well. Cover and simmer until the rice is tender, about 20 minutes.

Cut four slices off the lemon and juice the rest into the soup. Stir in the chickpeas. Remove the spice mixture and the cinnamon stick.

Season with black pepper to taste and ladle into warmed bowls. Garnish with mint leaves and lemon slices, and add hot sauce to taste.

Yield: 4 servings

Heat Scale: Mild to Medium

Yellow Pepper Soup with Orange Habaneros

Here's a trip to the Caribbean, where vegetable soups like calaloo are very popular. Serve this with one of the rice dishes in Chapter 5 for a complete meal.

2   tablespoons olive oil

4   leeks, white and light green parts only, washed and thinly sliced

6   yellow bell peppers, seeds removed, chopped

1   habanero chile, seeds and stem removed, chopped

6   large sprigs fresh tarragon

3   cups Super-Rich Vegetable Stock (see recipe, p. 4)

Salt and pepper

Tarragon leaves

Olive oil

Cayenne Croutons (see recipe, p. 9)

Heat the olive oil in a pot, add the leeks, and sauté for about 10 minutes. Add the bell peppers, habanero, tarragon, and stock and bring to a boil. Reduce the heat and simmer until the peppers are very tender, about 20 minutes. Add the salt and pepper to taste and stir well.

Remove from the heat and discard the tarragon sprigs. Transfer to a food processor and puree. Strain the puree through a sieve and return it to the pot for reheating.

Serve in bowls garnished with the tarragon leaves and a drizzle of olive oil, topped with Cayenne Croutons.

Yield: 4 servings

Heat Scale: Hot

Sopa de Tortilla

Here's another soup from Nancy Gerlach, who really assisted on this chapter. She loves Mexico so much, she's there at least twice a year collecting recipes. She wrote in *Chile Pepper* magazine: "Tortilla strips can be served as croutons in soups, as in this recipe, or in salads. This soup can be a thin broth, or thick with vegetables, but always add the tortilla strips right before serving so they don't get soggy. The fried pasillas were served at a small restaurant in Cozumel as a condiment to some cruise folks, and they make a great addition to the soup."

	Vegetable oil for frying
4	corn tortillas, cut in strips
1	small onion, chopped
2	cloves garlic, chopped
3	jalapeño chiles, stems and seeds removed, chopped
2	tomatoes, peeled, seeds removed, chopped
1	sprig epazote (optional)
½	teaspoon dried oregano

4	cups Super-Rich Vegetable Stock (see recipe, p. 4)
4	whole dried pasilla chiles
	Chopped fresh cilantro
	Grated Monterey Jack cheese or crumbled queso fresco
	Diced avocado
	Sour cream
	Lime wedges

Pour the oil in a pan to a depth of 2 inches. Fry the tortilla strips, a few at a time, until they are golden. Remove, drain well, and save the oil.

Sauté the onion and garlic in a teaspoon of the oil until they are soft. Add the jalapeños and sauté for an additional minute. Add the tomatoes, epazote, oregano, and 1 cup of the stock. Simmer the mixture for 10 minutes.

Place the mixture in a blender or food processor and puree until it is smooth. Strain the mixture if desired. Combine the puree with the remaining stock and simmer for 20 minutes.

Reheat the reserved oil and fry the whole pasilla chiles until they start to crisp. Remove and drain.

To serve: Divide the tortilla strips into individual soup bowls, ladle the hot soup over them, and garnish with the cilantro. Serve the cheese, avocado, sour cream, and lime wedges as garnishes, including the whole fried pasillas, on the side.

Yield: 4 servings

Heat Scale: Medium

The Skinny on Potatoes

"Raw potato skins have about the same nutrient content of the raw tuber, with slightly higher levels of calcium and zinc. Baking potatoes, however, causes more vitamins to accumulate in the skin. They are also a good source of fiber. So, Mom was kind of right about making you eat your skins. One thing Mom probably didn't know is that potato peels may contain a naturally occurring poison, solanine. A greening of the potato skin is a telltale sign of too much solanine. Don't panic—just don't eat any green-skinned potatoes."

Don Voorhees

Three-Mushroom, Two-Chile Soup

It's wonderful that there's such a variety of both mushrooms and chiles available these days, so why not combine them into a uniquely flavorful soup? Serve with a toasted bread from Chapter 8.

3	ounces dried shiitake mushrooms	2	cloves garlic, minced
5	cups cold Super-Rich Vegetable Stock (see recipe, p. 4)	1	pound white mushrooms, thinly sliced
3	tablespoons olive oil	¼	cup minced Italian parsley
2	small leeks, white part only, thinly sliced	1	tablespoon ground New Mexican red chile
½	cup chopped onion		Salt and pepper
4	small red potatoes, peeled and thinly sliced	¼	cup dry sherry
			Enoki mushrooms
½	cup roasted, peeled, and chopped New Mexican green chile		Italian parsley leaves

Soak the dried mushrooms in 2 cups of the stock for 30 minutes, then drain. Reserve the mushrooms. Strain the stock back into the remaining stock and set aside.

In a large saucepan, heat the oil and add the leeks, onion, potatoes, green chile, and garlic. Sauté over medium heat, stirring often, for 10 minutes. Add the white mushrooms and parsley and continue to sauté for 7 minutes. Add the reserved mushrooms and the stock and bring to a boil.

Reduce the heat, add the red chile, cover, and simmer for 30 minutes over low heat. Add the salt and pepper to taste.

Transfer half of the soup to a blender and puree in batches. Return the puree to the saucepan and mix well. Add the sherry just before serving and mix well.

Serve garnished with the enoki mushrooms and parsley leaves.

Yield: 6 servings

Heat Scale: Medium

Chipotle Black Bean Soup with Pumpkin

What is it about the combination of black beans and chipotle chiles? Mary Jane's fondness for black beans collides with Dave's love of chipotles in this hearty soup. It takes a bit of time to cook the beans, but after that it's a snap.

1 pound black beans	¼ cup vegetable oil
1 teaspoon salt	1½ cups finely chopped onions
¾ cup drained canned tomatoes	3 cloves garlic, peeled and crushed
1 cup canned pumpkin puree	1 teaspoon ground cumin
3 chipotle chiles, rehydrated (by soaking in hot water for an hour) and chopped	¼ cup red wine vinegar
	½ cup medium sherry
3 cups Super-Rich Vegetable Stock (see recipe, p. 4)	Cilantro leaves

In a large saucepan, place the beans, enough water to cover plus 2 inches, and the salt. Bring to a boil, partially cover the pan, reduce the heat, and simmer until the beans are tender, 1½ to 2 hours. Drain the beans.

Stir the tomatoes into the beans and transfer to a food processor. Pulse briefly, leaving the beans somewhat chunky. Return the beans and tomatoes to the saucepan and stir in the pumpkin, chipotles, and half of the stock. Bring to a simmer.

Heat the oil over medium heat in a saucepan. Add the onions and sauté for about 8 minutes, then add the garlic and cumin and stir well. Add this onion mixture to the beans, stir in the remaining stock and the vinegar, and simmer for 15 minutes. Adjust the consistency by adding sherry, and stir well.

Serve garnished with the cilantro leaves.

Yield: 4 to 6 servings

Heat Scale: Medium

Note: This recipe requires advance preparation.

Mushroom and Barley Soup with Hot Paprika

This chunky soup from Europe is virtually a stew (the lines sometimes blur), depending on how much of the vegetable stock you add. Be sure to use imported Hungarian paprika rather than the American versions. If the paprika is not hot enough, mix it with some ground red New Mexican chile powder.

1	cup barley	½	cup finely chopped Italian parsley
½	cup vegetable oil		
1	pound parsnips, scraped and chopped fine	2	large cloves garlic, peeled and crushed
1	pound carrots, scraped and chopped fine	6	cups Super-Rich Vegetable Stock (see recipe, p. 4)
4	cups chopped onions	2	cups light cream
¼	cup hot paprika	3	tablespoons lemon juice
2½	pounds white mushrooms, wiped		Salt and pepper

Bring 4 cups of water to boil in a pot. Add the barley, cover, reduce the heat, and simmer until tender, about 25 minutes. Drain and reserve.

Heat the oil in a large, heavy saucepan, add the parsnips, carrots, and onions and stir well. Add the paprika and stir again. Cover and cook over low heat, stirring occasionally, for 10 minutes.

Reserve about ½ pound of mushrooms. Place the remaining mushrooms in a food processor and pulse until finely minced. Add the minced mushrooms and the Italian parsley to the vegetables and continue cooking for 5 minutes, stirring occasionally. Stir in the garlic and cook for 2 more minutes.

Cut the remaining mushrooms into thin slices and add them, the reserved barley, stock, cream, and lemon juice. Add the salt and pepper to taste. Simmer the soup for 15 minutes and serve.

Yield: 8 to 10 servings

Heat Scale: Mild

North of the Border Vegetable Chowder

The Southwestern chile flavor is here—just in chowder form! We've tried to keep the fat content way down while the taste is way up, so use reduced-fat sharp cheddar cheese. This chowder can easily be spiced up by adding some red chile powder along with the mustard and marjoram.

3 tablespoons olive oil	¼ teaspoon dried marjoram
2 cups chopped onions	2 cups corn kernels
½ cup diced celery	½ cup grated reduced-fat sharp cheddar cheese, plus a little for garnish
½ cup diced carrots	
½ cup diced red bell pepper	
½ cup diced green bell pepper	½ cup roasted, peeled, and chopped New Mexican green chiles, or more to taste
2 tablespoons flour	
5 cups Super-Rich Vegetable Stock (see recipe, p. 4)	
	Salt and pepper
3 cups diced potatoes	Cilantro leaves
1 teaspoon dry mustard	

Heat the oil in a large pot, add the onions, celery, carrots, and bell peppers and sauté, stirring frequently, for 7 to 10 minutes, or until the onions are soft. Stir in the flour and cook for 1 minute.

Add the stock, potatoes, mustard, and marjoram, stir well, and bring to a boil. Reduce the heat to low, cover, and simmer for 10 minutes. Stir in the corn and simmer for 4 minutes more or until the potatoes are done.

Transfer 2 cups of the stew with vegetables to a blender and add ¼ cup cheese. Puree until smooth. Transfer to another pot. Repeat with the remaining stew and cheese.

Add the green chile and simmer, stirring frequently, for about 5 minutes, taking care that the soup doesn't boil. Add salt and pepper to taste.

To serve, ladle into warm bowls and garnish with the extra cheese and cilantro leaves.

Yield: 6 servings

Heat Scale: Mild

Split Pea–Poblano Stew

Here's our thick and spicy variation on split pea soup without ham or any other meat product. It's also great with green New Mexican chiles. Serve with toasted pita points or a bread from Chapter 8.

2 tablespoons olive oil	½ teaspoon thyme
1 onion, diced	1 carrot, chopped
1 bay leaf	3 ribs celery, chopped
1 teaspoon celery seed	½ cup chopped Italian parsley
1 cup green split peas	1 potato, peeled and diced
¼ cup barley	2 poblano chiles, roasted, peeled, seeds and stems removed, chopped
½ cup lima beans	
10 cups Super-Rich Vegetable Stock (see recipe, p. 4)	Salt and pepper
½ teaspoon basil	

In a large soup kettle, heat the olive oil. Add the onion, bay leaf, and celery seed and sauté until the onion is soft. Add the peas, barley, lima beans, and stock and cook, covered, over low heat for 1 hour and 20 minutes. Stir occasionally.

   Add the basil, thyme, carrot, celery, parsley, potato, and chiles. Turn the heat down very low, and simmer, covered, for 30 to 45 minutes or until the potato is soft. Stir occasionally, and add more stock if the stew gets too thick. Add the salt and pepper to taste.

Yield: 6 to 8 servings

Heat Scale: Mild

Indian-Style Lentil and Chile Stew

Here is a hearty vegetarian stew with plenty of spices, so it could even be called a curried stew. Serve it with Indian *naan* bread or even pita bread and a salad from Chapter 3. To make an even thicker presentation, serve this over 1 cup of cooked rice in a large bowl.

3	cups dried lentils	12	whole cloves
1	teaspoon salt	2	sticks cinnamon
1	tablespoon cumin seed	12	green cardamom pods
1	tablespoon poppy seed	3	cups grated coconut
2	tablespoons ground New Mexican red chile	12	cloves garlic
		½	cup canola oil
2	tablespoons coriander seed	6	onions, sliced

In a saucepan, cover the lentils with water and bring to a boil. Reduce the heat, cover, and simmer for 45 minutes. When they are done, remove from the heat and stir in the salt.

While the lentils are cooking, heat the cumin seed, poppy seed, chile, coriander, cloves, cinnamon sticks, and cardamom pods in a heavy skillet over low heat, stirring well, until they are heated and fragrant. Take care not to burn them. Place the mixture in a spice mill or coffee grinder and grind it to a powder.

In a food processor, combine the spice mixture with the coconut and garlic and puree. Heat the canola oil in a skillet and fry the onions until golden. Add the spice mixture and fry for 3 or 4 minutes, stirring constantly.

Transfer the fried mixture to the lentils, stir well, and simmer for 10 minutes, adding more water if necessary.

Yield: 6 servings

Heat Scale: Medium

White Bean Stew with Spicy Olivada Sauce

This hearty, spicy stew has a Mediterranean feel because of the *olivada* sauce that is served over the top. To make *olivada*, simply puree pitted black olives with enough olive oil to make a smooth paste. Serve this with a toasted bread from Chapter 8 and a salad from Chapter 3 for a great chilehead brunch.

Sauce:

1	garlic clove, minced
1	teaspoon minced rosemary
1½	teaspoons *olivada*
½	teaspoon chiltepin or other very hot chile powder
4	tablespoons olive oil

Combine all sauce ingredients in a bowl and mix well. Cover and reserve.

Stew:

2	cups dried white beans, cleaned and rinsed
1	carrot, diced
1	onion, sliced thin
10	medium plum tomatoes, peeled and quartered
2	medium potatoes, peeled and diced
2	tablespoons minced Italian parsley
½	cup chopped New Mexican green chile
2	cups Super-Rich Vegetable Stock (see recipe, p. 4)
	Salt and pepper

Put the beans in a large pot, cover with cold water, and bring to a boil. Cover, remove from the heat, and let sit for 1 hour.

Drain the beans and return to the pot. Add the carrot, onion, tomatoes, potatoes, parsley, green chile, and stock. Bring to a boil, partially cover, reduce heat, and simmer until the beans are tender, about 1 to 1½ hours. Stir occasionally. Add more stock if the stew gets too thick. Add salt and pepper to taste.

To serve, ladle into warm bowls and drizzle each portion with 1 teaspoon (or more) *olivada* sauce.

Yield: 6 servings

Heat Scale: Medium

Note: This recipe requires advance preparation.

Great Soup Quotes

"Of soup and love, the first is best."

Spanish proverb

"Of all the items on the menu, soup is that which exacts the most delicate perfection and the strictest attention."

Escoffier

"Beautiful soups! Who cares for fish, game, or any other dish? Who would not give all else for two pennyworth only of beautiful soup?"

Lewis Carroll

"Cold soup is a very tricky thing and it is the rare hostess who can carry it off. More often than not the dinner guest is left with the impression that had he only come a little earlier, he could have gotten it while it was still hot."

Fran Liebowitz

The Grains of Paradise and Lively Legumes

Grains are more properly classified as cereal grains, because cereal includes any plant from the grass family that yields an edible grain or seed. Wheat and barley cultivation was evident 10,000 years ago in the Middle East. The ancient Greeks worshipped Demeter, the goddess of agriculture, and ancient Romans worshipped Ceres, from whose name we get cereal. In Japan, the mythic figure representing abundance is called the Great Grain Spirit. You just can't escape references to grains because of their importance to civilization and survival.

One of the most commonly consumed grains, rice, comprises the first set of recipes. Because rice is so prevalent, we think that just about every person in the world has eaten rice in one form or another; however, unless they buy our cookbook, they won't experience our uncommon approach to this common grain. If you are from the northern Midwest, you have probably eaten wild rice—with butter or an even blander cream sauce. We jazz up the rice in Wild West Wild Rice Combo (p. 115). This recipe uses some everyday ingredients that are brought together in an unusual way. The nutty taste of the rice is further enhanced with chopped nuts and an infusion of chipotle chiles.

Since hot and spicy is the name of the game, we have added one more element to the next three recipes—ease of preparation. Racy Rice and Vegetable Stir-Fry (p. 116) combines fresh ginger, serrano chiles, and crunchy vegetables to this delectable side dish. Louisiana inspired us to create Spicy Creole Rice (p. 117) with the holy triad of bell peppers, onions, and tomatoes—and a hefty infusion of cayenne. This recipe is so good that we always want to make a pot of gumbo after eating it. The last rice recipe, as well as the spiciest, is Arroz Diablo, or Devil Rice (p. 118). This recipe is truly the work of the gourmet devil—one with a penchant for good food that is also hot and spicy.

The delicious Serrano, Grain, and Mushroom Pilaf (p. 119) contains two tasty grains: barley and brown rice. Brown rice adds a slightly nutty flavor and a chewy texture, while the portobello mushrooms give the dish a substantial, meaty texture. Spicy Southwest Barley and Sweet Potatoes (p. 120) has the unusual combination of fennel seeds, sweet potatoes, green chile, and an infusion of tomatillos, which are sometimes called Mexican green tomatoes. Cooking enhances the flavor of the tomatillo, which melds well with the lemon and herbs.

And speaking of bringing out the flavor, we have included two recipes for couscous, an underutilized dish here in the U.S. Couscous is granular semolina, a type of cracked wheat, and it has the unique ability to absorb a variety of flavors from different ingredients. Also, couscous can be cooked in about five minutes—a quick base for some of the grilled entrees. Golden Green Chile Couscous with Dates (p. 121) contrasts the flavors of chiles and dates— it's hot and semisweet at the same time. We like to vary the traditional tabbouleh recipe by substituting couscous for bulgur. Tantalizing Tomato Couscous Tabbouleh (p. 122) is one example. It differs from the usual recipe with the addition of cayenne, fresh basil, and Parmesan cheese, and all of these ingredients produce a refreshing dish that can be served as an appetizer with romaine lettuce, a side dish, or a sandwich stuffed in pita bread.

Another wheat-based recipe is Habanero, Bulgur, and Mango Piñon Pilaf (p. 123). Bulgur wheat makes an excellent pilaf, and the addition of the mango and chile will please your taste buds. Cascabel, Wheat Berry, and Barley Salad (p. 124) plays off the tastes of hot, sour, sweet, and smoky with its cascabel chiles, balsamic vinegar, mandarin oranges, and smoked cheese. The cheese will melt somewhat and bind some of the ingredients, thus assuring you of vibrant flavor with every bite.

Except in the South, grits are another underutilized item. Our Chile Cheese Grits Casserole (p. 125) is rich with cheese and red chile, and using low-fat cheese will not change the taste or texture. If a little sweetness won't conflict with the rest of your dinner, try serving this dish with red chile honey. Since polenta is making a comeback on Italian restaurant menus, we have included two recipes here that have a little more punch than the average polenta recipe. Cheese-Chile Polenta (p. 126) is laced with jalapeños, sun-dried tomatoes, pepper cheese, and cilantro. This recipe turns up the heat— you may want to serve it with one of the milder entrees so the flavors won't fight each other. The next polenta recipe is sauced and saucy. Red Chile Polenta with Primavera Jalapeño Sauce (p. 128) is an elegant side dish to serve; it is especially good with grilled portobello mushrooms.

Beans or legumes are the mature seeds that grow inside pods, and these "seeds" can be made into some of the most delicious dishes. Our ancestors must have realized this fact as well, because beans have been cultivated for at least 4,000 years. Since beans are so easy to grow and store, it is no wonder that they are a major food staple in various parts of the world wherever animal protein is in short supply. We are sure that these delicious recipes will convert your nonbean-eating friends who still remember the campfire scene from *Blazing Saddles.*

Entice them first with Baked Black Beans with Quinoa and Corn (p. 130), which includes the nutritious grain quinoa. The dish is spiced with the habanero chile; other flavors include ground cloves, thyme, oregano, and cumin, all of which bake into the beans and quinoa. Black beans get yet another treatment in Red Hot Hummus (p. 127), in which they are combined with red wine vinegar, garlic, ground red chile, and fresh cilantro. Serve the hummus with pita bread or on Bibb lettuce leaves to accompany one of the entrees from Chapter 6.

Hearty White Beans with Chipotle Chiles (p. 132) have a subtle smoky taste that comes from the chipotle chiles, or smoked jalapeños. The complementary tastes and colors come from bell peppers, tomatoes, kalamata olives, and artichoke hearts. The final bean recipe, Not the Usual Baked Beans (p. 134), is a new twist on the traditional Boston baked beans. Because Puritans were forbidden to cook on the Sabbath, the bean pot was created so the beans could slow-cook all night and be ready for Sunday. Our baked beans still require a long and slow cooking—not for religious reasons, but to infuse and meld all of the flavors.

The next set of recipes are all different and tasty; we like to experiment with traditional grains, fruits, vegetables, and spices in unique combinations. Some of these recipes were created by simply using what we had on hand to create a satisfying dish. Pungent Quinoa with Fruit (p. 133) was created when we had bits and pieces of fruit left over as well as leftover quinoa; add one thawed habanero chile, and a dish was born. This fruity dish goes well with grilled vegetables. Macaroni with Swiss Chard and Garlic Cayenne Bean Sauce (p. 136) is a satisfying main dish or side dish utilizing cannellini beans, which are large, white Italian kidney beans. The garlic, cayenne, chard, and oregano add the heat and the flavor to this recipe.

Lentils, another staple food used as a meat substitute in parts of Europe and through much of the Middle East and India, is often maligned visually and gastronomically. They have been given unappealing descriptions because of their appearance: "They look like remnants of a large machine-tooling project," says essayist Jon Carroll, who has probably never tried our Lentil, Serrano, and Jicama Salad (p. 137). This lentil salad gets its crunch from jicama and fresh serrano chiles and is sauced with a hefty infusion of garlic, red wine vinegar, and feta cheese.

After cooking all of our bean recipes, just remember that there are more than seventy different varieties of legumes. And, if you start to get gastro-feedback, try reading Robert Burton's book published in 1621, *The Anatomy of Melancholy*. He offers sixty-four remedies to abolish this problem.

Wild West Wild Rice Combo

Wild rice has such great flavor and texture that we all cook with it more. It is expensive, but a little bit goes a long way, and cooked brown rice can be added to extend the dish. Actually, this "rice" is a long-grain marsh grass that was first harvested by the Native Americans of the northern Great Lakes area.

½ teaspoon salt
¾ cup wild rice
1 teaspoon dried thyme
2 tablespoons chopped chipotle chiles in adobo sauce
½ cup chopped pecans or walnuts
1 cup broccoli florets

1 cup chopped carrots
1 tablespoon canola or olive oil
1 cup chopped onion
1 cup chopped celery

Bring 1½ cups of water to a boil and add the salt. Wash the rice and pour it into the water, then add the thyme and the chipotles. When the mixture comes to a boil again, reduce the heat, cover, and cook for 35 to 45 minutes, until all the liquid has been absorbed.

Meanwhile, lightly toast the pecans or walnuts in a 350-degree oven for 5 to 8 minutes; check the progress, as they burn easily.

Steam the broccoli and the carrots; drain and set aside.

Heat the oil in a medium skillet and sauté the onion and the celery until the onion starts to wilt, about 1 minute. Set aside.

When the rice is done, fluff it up with a fork, add the pecans, broccoli, carrots, and the sautéed mixture, and toss lightly. Cover tightly and reheat only until it is hot. Serve immediately.

Yield: 4 servings

Heat Scale: Medium

Racy Rice and Vegetable Stir Fry

Some chopping is involved in this recipe, but the process goes quickly because it is in small quantities. The vegetables add just the right amount of texture and color to this rice dish. Basmati rice will add the unique flavor that completes this rice dish.

2	tablespoons chile oil, or 2 tablespoons grapeseed oil and ½ teaspoon coarsely ground red chile	3	serrano chiles, seeds and stems removed, thinly sliced
½	cup broccoli florets	¼	cup chopped jicama or water chestnuts
2	tablespoons coarsely chopped red bell pepper	¼	cup snow peas or sugar snap peas
¼	cup chopped scallions	½	cup bean sprouts
1	teaspoon grated fresh ginger	2	cups cooked basmati rice
2	cloves garlic, minced	2	ounces straw mushrooms

Heat the oil in a wok or a large skillet and quickly sauté the broccoli, bell pepper, scallions, ginger, garlic, chiles, jicama, and snow peas, stirring frequently to avoid burning.

Add the bean sprouts and the cooked rice, and toss it with the vegetables. Add the mushrooms to one side of the wok to heat, then lightly toss the entire mixture. Serve immediately.

Yield: 4 to 6 servings

Heat Scale: Medium

Spicy Creole Rice

Using Super-Rich Vegetable Stock to cook the rice adds flavor as well as additional nutrients. The heat in this dish comes from cayenne pepper, and the amount can be adjusted up or down, according to your tastes.

1 tablespoon canola oil	1 teaspoon dried thyme
1 cup diced onion	1 teaspoon cayenne powder
½ cup diced green or red bell pepper	2 cups Super-Rich Vegetable Stock (see recipe, p. 4)
1 cup white rice	½ cup frozen peas, thawed and drained
1 teaspoon salt	
1 large tomato, seeded, drained, and chopped	

Heat the oil in a small saucepan and sauté the onion, bell pepper, rice, and salt until the onion wilts. Add the tomato, thyme, cayenne, and stock and bring the mixture to a boil. Reduce the heat, cover, and simmer for 20 to 25 minutes, until the liquid has evaporated. Remove the pot from the heat.

Toss the peas into the cooked rice, cover, and serve in 5 minutes.

Yield: 4 servings

Heat Scale: Medium

Arroz Diablo (Devil Rice)

This recipe was graciously offered by our friends at the Stonewall Chile Pepper Company, who make some of the hottest and most flavorful salsa around. We suggest its use in this recipe; however, feel free to substitute another salsa if you're in a pinch.

2 cups long-grain white rice
3 tablespoons olive oil
1 medium onion, chopped
2 cloves garlic, peeled and chopped

1 cup Salsa Del Diablo (or substitute other habanero salsa)
4 cups Super-Rich Vegetable Stock (see recipe, p. 4)
   Salt

Sauté the rice in the olive oil in a large pan until it begins to color. Add the onion and garlic and stir until the rice is a golden brown, being careful not to burn.

Add the Salsa Del Diablo and 1 cup of the stock, and simmer for about 5 minutes. Add the remaining stock, cover the pan with a tight-fitting lid, and simmer until the liquid is absorbed, about 20 minutes.

Yield: 4 servings

Heat Scale: Hot

Serrano, Grain, and Mushroom Pilaf

Barley can be traced back to the Stone Age, but in this recipe it gets a jazzy update with some crunchy vegetables and some spice from the chile. Serve this dish with one of the spicy salads from Chapter 3.

2	tablespoons chile oil, or 2 tablespoons olive oil with ½ teaspoon pure red ground chile	1⅔	cups Super-Rich Vegetable Stock (see recipe, p. 4)
⅓	cup pearl barley	1	tablespoon olive oil
⅓	cup long-grain brown rice	¼	pound portobello mushrooms, cleaned and chopped
2	serrano or jalapeño chiles, seeds and stems removed, diced	¼	cup chopped red or green bell pepper
½	cup chopped shallots	¾	cup chopped and drained fresh tomatoes
¼	cup minced celery	3	tablespoons chopped cilantro or Italian parsley
½	teaspoon dried Mexican oregano		

Heat the chile oil in a small heavy saucepan, add the barley, rice, serranos, shallots, celery, and oregano, and lightly sauté the mixture for 3 minutes, stirring and tossing. Add the stock and bring to a boil, then reduce the heat, cover, and simmer for 35 to 45 minutes, or until the rice and barley are cooked and the liquid is absorbed.

Meanwhile, in a small skillet, heat the olive oil, add the mushrooms, and sauté for 1 minute, stirring occasionally.

When the rice-barley mixture is done, stir in the sautéed mushrooms, bell peppers, tomatoes, and cilantro or parsley. Toss the mixture and serve.

Yield: 4 servings

Heat Scale: Medium

Spicy Southwest Barley and Sweet Potatoes

The familiar barley gets a new treatment here; it is combined with sweet potatoes and a shot of New Mexican green chile, the vitamin C content of this dish. It has taste, texture, and crunch.

2 tablespoons olive oil	¼ cup chopped tomatillos
2 teaspoons fennel seeds	½ cup diced New Mexican green chile
1 teaspoon crushed cumin seeds	
2 cups diced sweet potatoes, cut into ½-inch cubes	1 cup quick-cooking barley
1 teaspoon salt	2 cups Super-Rich Vegetable Stock (see recipe, p. 4)
¼ teaspoon freshly ground white pepper	¼ cup chopped jicama or water chestnuts
¼ cup chopped celery	

Heat the olive oil in a medium skillet, add the fennel seeds and cumin seeds, and stir for 15 seconds. Add the sweet potatoes, salt, pepper, and celery and sauté for 15 minutes, stirring frequently.

Add the tomatillos, green chile, barley, and the stock and bring the mixture to a boil. Reduce the heat, cover, and simmer for 15 minutes. Check the liquid and add more if necessary, to keep the mixture moist. Stir in the jicama and serve.

Yield: 3 to 4 servings

Heat Scale: Medium

Golden Green Chile Couscous with Dates

If you like textured food, you'll love this recipe. The combination of dates, green chile, and shallots guarantee a sweet yet slightly fiery taste delight.

2	tablespoons orange juice		1½	cups couscous
1	tablespoon olive oil		½	cup chopped dates
½	teaspoon salt		½	cup chopped shallots
⅛	teaspoon ground cumin		2	green chiles, roasted, seeded, and chopped
2	cups water			

In a saucepan, bring the orange juice, oil, salt, cumin, and water to a boil. Stir in the couscous and dates. Remove from the heat and cover. Let the couscous stand until all the water is absorbed. Fluff the couscous with a fork, then stir in the shallots and green chiles and serve.

Yield: 4 large servings

Heat Scale: Medium

Tantalizing Tomato Couscous Tabbouleh

This dish is a staple of North Africa, although many countries have their own version of this recipe; Moroccans include saffron, and Algerians add tomatoes. We've even included a touch of Tunisia by spicing things up.

1½	cups couscous	½	cup basil leaves, finely chopped
2	teaspoons olive oil	3	shallots, coarsely chopped
½	teaspoon salt	2	large tomatoes, seeded and chopped
2	teaspoons cayenne powder		
2	cups boiling water	½	cup fresh lime juice
1½	cups parsley, finely chopped	2	tablespoons Parmesan cheese

In a large bowl, combine the couscous, oil, salt, and cayenne. Pour the boiling water over the couscous mixture, cover, and let it stand until the water is absorbed. After about 5 minutes, fluff the couscous with a fork, then let it stand until it is at room temperature.

Toss the parsley, basil, shallots, tomatoes, and lime juice into the couscous. Sprinkle the cheese on top and serve.

Yield: 4 to 6 servings

Heat Scale: Medium

Habanero, Bulgur, and Mango Piñon Pilaf

We call habaneros and mangos the dynamic duo, as their flavors perfectly complement one another. In India, mangos are known as the fruits of the gods—we would have to agree!

1   small onion, finely chopped
¼   teaspoon minced fresh habanero
1   cup plus 2 tablespoons Super-Rich Vegetable Stock (see recipe, p. 4)

½   cup chopped mango
¾   cup bulgur
3   tablespoons roasted piñons (pine nuts)
1   teaspoon minced garlic

In a small heavy saucepan, cook the onion and habanero until the onions are soft. Stir in the stock, mango, and bulgur and bring the mixture to a boil. Cover the pan and cook for 10 to 12 minutes, or until the liquid is absorbed.

Remove the pan from the heat and let the pilaf stand, covered, for 5 minutes. Stir in the piñons and garlic and serve.

Yield: 4 cups

Heat Scale: Hot

The Hottest Man in the World

Japan's hot food eating champion is Morihiro Yamashita, who won a televised contest by eating hot noodles and curried rice spiced with 120 times the usual amount of chile. According to news reports, Yamashita felt faint during the noodle round and in the curry round his tongue went numb and he briefly lost his eyesight—but he eventually won the big, well, chile.

Cascabel, Wheat Berry, and Barley Salad

We've spiced up this healthy dish with the addition of cascabels, which offer a rich, hot taste. You can feel great after you make this salad; the barley will help lower your blood pressure as well as nourish your nerve cells and calcify the bones.

1	cup wheat berries	½	cup mandarin oranges, chopped
1	cup pearl barley	½	pound smoked Gouda cheese, diced
3	cascabels, stems and seeds removed, minced	3	roma tomatoes, chopped
1	red onion, finely chopped	½	cup chopped fresh shallots
2	garlic cloves, minced	1	teaspoon lime juice
¼	cup balsamic vinegar	1	teaspoon lemon juice
¼	cup olive oil		
6	chives, chopped		

Add the wheat berries to a large kettle of boiling water and cook at a slow boil for 30 minutes. Stir in the barley and cook the grains together for another 40 minutes.

While the grains are cooking, combine the cascabels, onion, garlic, vinegar, oil, and chives in a mixing bowl. Drain the grains, and add them to the onion mixture. Add the oranges, cheese, tomatoes, shallots, lime juice, and lemon juice and mix well.

Yield: 6 servings

Heat Scale: Medium

Chile Cheese Grits Casserole

This dish is a classic case of a dish from the South meeting the Southwest. It is a rich dish and is best served with something simple. Since grits refers to any coarsely ground grain such as corn, oats, or rice, it is important that you use corn grits in this recipe.

1½	cups corn grits	3	eggs, or 1 egg plus ½ cup egg substitute
6	cups boiling water	1	teaspoon salt
1	teaspoon salt	1	teaspoon paprika
6	tablespoons butter	3	teaspoons pure red ground chile, such as Chimayo
1	cup grated low-fat Jarlsberg cheese		
1	cup grated low-fat sharp cheddar cheese		

Preheat the oven to 325 degrees.

Pour the grits in the boiling water, add salt, and simmer for 30 minutes. (If you are using instant grits, follow the directions on the package.) Remove the grits from the heat, add the butter and cheeses, and stir until the butter is melted.

Beat the eggs and add to the grits, along with the salt, paprika, and red chile. Mix well. Spread the mixture in a lightly oiled casserole and bake for 1 hour. If the top starts to brown too quickly, cover the pan with aluminum foil.

Yield: 6 servings

Heat Scale: Mild

Cheese-Chile Polenta

We are taking the liberty of including a corn recipe here, only because it is so delicious, and it really didn't fit into the vegetable chapter. What can we say? Make it—you'll love it!

3	tablespoons chile oil	2	cups cornmeal
2	cloves garlic, minced	3	sun-dried tomatoes, rehydrated and minced
4	jalapeño or serrano chiles, seed and stems removed, minced	2	cups grated pepper-Jack cheese or low-fat Jarlsberg cheese
1	ancho chile, toasted, rehydrated, and minced	3	tablespoons chopped cilantro
1	teaspoon salt	½	cup low-fat milk
8½	cups boiling water		

Heat the chile oil in a small skillet and sauté the garlic and chiles for 30 seconds, stirring so that the garlic doesn't burn. Remove the pan from the heat and set aside.

Add the salt to the boiling water, then add the cornmeal in a slow, steady stream, whisking constantly to avoid lumping. Reduce the heat to a simmer and stir the cornmeal frequently for 10 minutes. Remove the mixture from the heat and stir in the reserved chile sauté, sun-dried tomatoes, 1½ cups of the cheese, cilantro, and milk and mix thoroughly. Pour the mixture into a greased 2½-quart baking dish, cover, and chill for 1 hour.

Preheat the oven to 350 degrees. Bake the polenta for 30 minutes, or until it is heated through. Remove from the oven, then change the oven setting to turn on the broiler. Sprinkle the top of the polenta with the remaining cheese and some red chile powder, if you wish.

Broil the polenta for 5 minutes, or until the top is bubbling. Remove the mixture and allow the polenta to sit for 10 minutes before serving.

Yield: 8 servings

Heat Scale: Hot

Note: This recipe requires advance preparation.

Red Hot Hummus

This is one of the most unique hummus recipes you will ever prepare; it's hot and rich tasting, and attractive all at the same time. Feel free to substitute flour tortilla strips for the pita bread.

2   (16-ounce) cans black beans
2   tablespoons olive oil
1   tablespoon soy sauce
1   tablespoon red wine vinegar
4   cloves garlic, chopped
½   lemon, juiced
1   tablepoon New Mexican red chile powder

1   tablespoon fresh cilantro, chopped
1   (16-ounce) can stewed tomatoes
3   scallions, chopped
4   pita breads, cut into triangles

Combine the black beans, olive oil, soy sauce, vinegar, garlic, lemon juice, red chile powder, and cilantro in a food processor. Fold in the stewed tomatoes and scallions. Serve on the pita bread.

Yield: 4 servings

Heat Scale: Medium

Red Chile Polenta with Primavera Jalapeño Sauce

This savory, low-fat recipe was created by Denice Skrepcinski. She says to vary the primavera sauce by using vegetables you have on hand or what's in season and fresh. For a more intense flavor, grill the vegetables for the sauce.

1   cup polenta
3   cups Super-Rich Vegetable Stock (see recipe, p. 4)
½   teaspoon red chile powder
3   tablespoons olive oil
½   cup chopped onion
3   cloves garlic, minced
1   jalapeño chile, seeds and stem removed, minced

2   cups mixed cooked, sliced vegetables, such as broccoli, zucchini, mushrooms, carrots, and squash
1   (28-ounce) can peeled Italian tomatoes, crushed in juice
     Cilantro or parsley

Combine the polenta and the stock in a large saucepan. Stir constantly over a high heat until the mixture is boiling. Reduce the heat and continue stirring until the polenta is thick enough to hold its shape. Stir in the red chile. Pour the mixture into a lightly greased 9-inch-square pan and spread evenly. Cover the mixture and chill for 2 hours.

Heat 2 tablespoons of the oil in a medium saucepan and add the onion, garlic, and chile and sauté until the onion is soft and translucent. Add the vegetables and tomatoes and their juice, reduce the heat, and allow the sauce to simmer for 10 to 15 minutes, until it is slightly thickened.

Cut the chilled polenta into 2½-inch squares, then cut the squares in half to form 2 triangles. Heat the remaining 1 tablespoon of olive oil in a large skillet and sauté the triangles until they are lightly browned and heated through.

Place 3 triangles on a warm plate and spoon the sauce over the triangles. Garnish with cilantro or parsley, if desired.

Yield: 4 to 6 servings

Heat Scale: Mild

Note: This recipe requires advance preparation.

Pod Pourri, Part 4

Moscow has its first Mexican restaurant, Azteca, atop the Intourist Hotel. . . . Word from Dr. Paul Bosland at The Chile Institute: at least two people have called asking for seeds for "chile penguin"; maybe that's "pequin". . . . Best chile-eating analogy of recent memory: "Ever notice how pretty the coloring is on a diamondback rattlesnake just before it bites you?"—Patrick Mott, *Los Angeles Times*. . . . According to the *Washington Post*, holistic veterinarian Sandy Bradley treats horses having chest ailments with hot pepper sauce; "Hot sauce is good for the circulatory system," she said. . . . The world's tallest jalapeño plant, grown by Fred and Josie Melton of Jacksonville, Florida, topped 12 feet, 3 inches and has yielded more than 1,700 pepper pods. . . .

Baked Black Beans with Quinoa and Corn

Black beans have always been popular in Mexico, Central and South America, and the Caribbean. They are becoming popular in the U.S. as well and are appearing on more and more menus. This hearty, spicy dish should be served hot from the casserole dish, and it would be a good accompaniment to one of the entrees in Chapter 6.

1	pound dried black beans, picked over and rinsed
2	tablespoons olive oil
1	cup chopped onion
¼	cup chopped celery
½	cup chopped red or yellow bell pepper
2	cloves garlic, minced
1	whole clove, ground in spice mill
1	teaspoon dried thyme
¾	teaspoon dried oregano
2	teaspoons chopped Italian parsley
½	teaspoon coarsely ground black pepper
1	teaspoon whole cumin seeds, crushed
1	habanero chile, seeds and stem removed, minced
1	teaspoon tamari sauce
2	to 2½ cups Super-Rich Vegetable stock (see recipe, p. 4)
½	cup quinoa
2	cups fresh or frozen corn, cooked and drained
1	cup chopped, drained tomatoes

Place the beans in a large, heavy casserole dish and cover with water 2 inches above the beans. Bring the beans to a boil and allow them to boil gently for 1 minute. Cover the beans and remove the pot from the heat. Let stand for 2 hours.

Drain the beans, then place them back into the cleaned casserole dish and cover with cold water. Bring the beans to a boil, reduce the heat to a simmer, cover, and simmer for 1 hour. Remove the beans from the heat, drain, and place back into the cleaned casserole dish.

Heat the oil in a skillet and sauté the onion, celery, bell pepper, garlic, ground clove, thyme, oregano, parsley, black pepper, cumin, habanero chile, and the tamari until the onion is wilted. Add the sautéed mixture to the beans and mix. Add enough of the stock to moisten, about 1 to 1½ cups. Cover and bake until the beans are tender, about 1 hour.

Cook the quinoa in the remaining 1 cup of stock in a covered saucepan, about 10 minutes, or until the liquid is absorbed. Fluff the quinoa with a fork, cover, and set aside.

When the beans are done, add the cooked quinoa, cooked corn, and tomatoes, mix, and serve.

Yield: 6 to 8 servings

Heat Scale: Medium

Note: This recipe requires advance preparation.

Bad Beans

"The ancient Greek philosopher Pythagoras had a great aversion to beans and forbade his followers from eating them. His aversion to the humble pulse arose from his belief that in eating beans one was devouring one's own parents, thereby causing great disruption to the cycle of reincarnation. . . . The English writer Henry Buttes banned beans on the grounds that they 'cause flatulencie, whereby they provoke to lechery'. . . . The bean's infamous tendency to cause flatulence means that this fine food is denied to jet fighter pilots and astronauts. As a pilot flies higher in an unpressurized cockpit, his intestinal gas expands."

Ross Leckie

Hearty White Beans with Chipotle Chiles

This white bean recipe could be a meal in itself, however, this colorful, spicy dish will add pizzazz to any meal; serve it with one of the entrees in Chapter 6. We think it is particularly good served hot, but it could also be served chilled.

1	pound dried white beans		1	(8-ounce) jar of water-packed artichoke hearts, drained and cut into quarters
2	tablespoons olive oil			
½	cup chopped onion		1	teaspoon dried basil
½	cup chopped green bell pepper		1	teaspoon salt
2	cloves garlic, minced		⅛	teaspoon freshly ground white pepper
2	chipotle chiles in adobo sauce			
¾	cup chopped plum tomatoes		¾	to 1 cup Super-Rich Vegetable Stock (see recipe, p. 4)
¼	cup sliced black kalamata olives			

Cook the beans according to the directions on the package, just until tender. Drain them thoroughly and pour them into a medium heavy saucepan.

Heat the oil in a skillet and sauté the onion, bell pepper, garlic, chipotles, and plum tomatoes just until the onion is translucent. Add this sautéed mixture to the beans, along with the olives, artichokes, basil, salt, pepper, and enough stock to moisten. Cover and heat the mixture for about 5 minutes. Serve immediately.

Yield: 6 servings

Heat Scale: Medium

Pungent Quinoa with Fruit

Quinoa is mountain grown—just like Juan Valdez's coffee! It is also another grain that some food researchers say is not really a grain; it is a dried fruit of the herb family, although the Incas did call it "the mother grain." In this recipe, it is combined with fruits and the habanero chile to give it taste and punch.

2½	cups Super-Rich Vegetable Stock (see recipe, p. 4)	½	cup chopped apple
1	cup quinoa	¼	cup chopped fresh apricots or rehydrated dried apricots
1	tablespoon olive or canola oil	½	teaspoon ground cinnamon
½	cup chopped onion	1	teaspoon orange zest
1	clove garlic, minced	½	cup currants
1	habanero chile, seeds and stem removed, minced		

Pour 2 cups of the stock into a saucepan and bring to a boil; add the quinoa, bring to a boil, reduce the heat to a simmer, cover, and simmer for 15 minutes. Remove from the heat, toss with a fork, cover, and set aside.

Heat the oil in a small saucepan and sauté the onion, garlic, chile, apple, apricots, and cinnamon for 1 minute, adding 1 tablespoon of the remaining stock.

Add the cooked quinoa to the sautéed mixture, along with the orange zest, currants, and the remaining stock. Simmer the mixture until it is just heated through. Serve immediately.

Yield: 6 to 8 servings

Heat Scale: Medium

Not the Usual Baked Beans

This is a dish that needs some precooking with the beans. Soaking the beans overnight is supposed to eliminate the gas factor! The addition of epazote will add a unique taste as well as help your digestive tract. The cooked beans freeze well.

1   pound dried pea beans or small navy beans, picked over and rinsed

1   teaspoon epazote (a common Mexican herb available in Latin Markets)

1   tablespoon olive oil

1   cup chopped onion

½   cup minced carrot

3   cloves garlic, minced

3   small sun-dried tomatoes, rehydrated and minced

1   (14-ounce) can stewed tomatoes, crushed

3   tablespoons soy bacon bits

¼   cup unsulferated molasses

1   tablespoon cider vinegar

1   teaspoon salt

2   ancho chiles, rehydrated, seeds and stems removed, pureed

1   teaspoon dry mustard

2   whole cloves, ground in a spice mill

Place the beans in a large heavy pot, cover with hot water, bring to a boil, and boil for 2 minutes. Remove the beans from the heat, cover, and let stand for 1 hour. Drain off the water, add enough cold water to cover, bring to a boil, reduce the heat to a simmer, cover, and cook until the beans are almost tender. The cooking time will vary, according to the altitude, but usually 1 to 2 hours. During the last 30 minutes of cooking, add the epazote.

Heat the oil in a skillet and sauté the onion, carrot, and garlic until the onion is wilted. Remove the pan from the heat and mix in the sun-dried tomatoes, stewed tomatoes, soy bits, molasses, vinegar, salt, ancho chiles, mustard, and cloves and stir.

Preheat the oven to 325 degrees. Place the beans and cooking liquid in a 3-quart ovenproof casserole. Stir the sautéed mixture into the beans and add water to barely cover the beans, if necessary.

Cover and bake for 1 hour. Remove the cover and continue baking for an additional 1½ hours. Add more water to keep the beans barely covered.

Yield: 6 servings

Heat Scale: Mild

Note: This recipe requires advance preparation.

He Has His Green Belt in Chile-Eating

"Just as I was helped in learning to be a chile lover by spending time around masters of the art, I am now able to help others. I have guided several people from the initial stages of mouth burning to intermediate and advanced levels of chile eating and am always gratified to watch them discover the joys of this practice and marvel at their newfound abilities. It is always uplifting to conquer something that seems unattainable. It is especially meaningful to see that by a change of mental attitude, perseverance, and openness to a new experience something that previously appeared painful and injurious can become pleasureful and beneficial."

Dr. Andrew Weil, author of *Spontaneous Healing*

Macaroni with Swiss Chard and Garlic Cayenne Bean Sauce

Swiss chard is available from April to December and is most plentiful between June and October. Although the leaves are its most prized feature, the stalks can also be cooked like asparagus.

6	tablespoons olive oil	¾	cup water
3	medium garlic cloves, minced	1	teaspoon dried oregano
2	shallots, minced	1	(16-ounce) can cannellini beans, drained
1	pound Swiss chard, leaves rinsed and cut into ½-inch-wide strips	2	teaspoons cayenne powder
		12	ounces macaroni

In a large skillet, heat the oil, add the garlic and shallots, then sauté about 1 minute. Add the Swiss chard and sauté until the leaves are wilted. Add the water, oregano, beans, and cayenne and cook over medium heat until the beans are heated and the sauce thickens slightly. Remove the sauce from the heat and cover to keep warm.

Boil 4 quarts of water in a large pot. Add the macaroni and cook until just tender, about 8 minutes. Drain the macaroni, then return it to the pot. Add the sauce, toss, and serve immediately.

Yield: 4 servings

Heat Scale: Medium

Lentil, Serrano, and Jicama Salad

One of the original meat substitutes, lentils are a great source of folic acid as well as lots of protein and fiber. Add that to the incredible amount of vitamin C in the serranos, and you've got a healthy and hot dish.

1	cup lentils	2	serrano chiles, seeds and stems removed, chopped
1	pound jicama, peeled and cubed	1½	teaspoons minced garlic
6	tablespoons olive oil	1	teaspoon minced tarragon
3	tablespoons red wine vinegar	½	cup feta cheese

Place the lentils in a saucepan and cover them with water. Boil the lentils until they are tender, about 18 minutes. Drain the lentils and let them cool to room temperature.

Place the jicama in a medium mixing bowl and whisk together the oil, vinegar, serranos, garlic, and tarragon. Gently mix in the lentils and feta cheese.

Yield: 4 servings

Heat Scale: Medium

Hurts So Good

The taste buds and nerve fibers in your mouth are so inter-twined that when you eat a hot chile, the chemical pain induced by the capsaicin is perceived as heat by the mouth and brain—and then as pleasure. So reports John Willoughby, writing in the *New York Times*.

In his article, Willoughby reports that studies by Dr. Barry Green at the Monell Chemical Senses Center in Philadelphia question the contention of chile haters that painful foods such as chiles and raw horseradish act as "gustatory sledge-hammers, reducing anything in which they are contained to one dimension by overpowering all other tastes." Dr. Green's experiments with such "masking" showed that this belief is not always true. "Some people were able to taste a variety of fla-vors after eating hot foods," Willoughby wrote, "but others were not."

But why? One theory from cognitive psychology holds that there are two kinds of people: holistic and analytical. When both eat hot and spicy food, the holistic people might believe that the food is too ridiculously hot to taste anything, while the other group "filters the taste through their analytical sensibility and responds, 'Wow, this is great. I can taste all these incredi-ble strong flavors.' " Dr. Green concluded: "The easiest expla-nation of why people like pain with their food is simply that it adds a whole new dimension to flavor."

Well, it seems that the pain-loving analyticals are gaining the edge over the holistics—the American Spice Trade Associ-ation reported that the consumption of red chile peppers rose by 25 percent in 1992. And in a telephone survey of 1,000 people nationwide conducted by the NRA (no guns—that's the National Restaurant Association), half of the people inter-viewed said that they liked their food very spicy rather than mildly spicy.

Pungent Pastas
and Main Dishes

Although it was believed for many years that Marco Polo brought the idea of noodles back with him to Italy after traveling to the Far East, the truth of the matter is that pasta was a player in the cuisines of the world before Marco Polo ever dreamed of spaghetti with marinara sauce. From German spaetzle to Polish pierogi, pastas have been a part of what's for dinner for centuries.

In the United States, pasta is more popular than ever; the National Pasta Association estimates that the average American now eats about twenty pounds of pasta a year. We've found pasta to be an awesome addition to a book dedicated to hot and spicy and meatless specialties. Since one cup of cooked pasta only contains a mere one gram of fat and 210 calories, it's the perfect meal when combined with the hot yet haute flavors of your favorite chiles.

Chile certainly plays an intricate part of our first recipe, Linguine with Pasilla, Cilantro, and Parsley Pesto (p. 143). This dish is packed full of the most heavenly herbs, including pasilla chiles, which add a hot, rich flavor to this interesting dish. Spicy, Urbane Mac and Cheese (p. 144) is not the usual macaroni and cheese. This dish gets its zip from habanero chiles, which is tempered by the cheeses and the herbs. Warning: this dish is not only habit-forming, it is also very rich. The flavored pasta used in this dish can be found in many large grocery stores and through mail order.

Our Red Hot Lover's Vegetarian Lo Mein (p. 146) proves that the old saying, "The quickest way to a person's heart is through their stomach," is still true. Recipe contributor Darryl Malloy reports that this dish seems to have a rather hot effect on his wife!

Pungent Pepper Oil from Chapter 1 is a main ingredient in our next recipe, Dan Dan Mein, or Dan Dan Noodles (p. 145). Direct from the Sichuan province of the People's Republic of China, this dish is one of the favorite snack foods in the country, enjoyed by everyone from workers to the elite.

Another recipe with a Chinese flair is Ballistic Baby Bok Choy and Fried Tofu (p. 148), which can be prepared in thirty minutes from start to finish. This dish combines different flavors and textures with the bok choy, chile, mushrooms, and water chestnuts. Spicy Sweet-and-Sour Tempeh (p. 150) is another entree that can be prepared in a flash. The contrast of flavors ranges from the sweetness of pineapple to the pizzazz of chiles and fresh ginger.

Terrific Tongue-Tingling Tofu Sloppy Joes (p. 152) is a new twist on an old favorite. Reporting on the President's diet, Hillary Rodham Clinton is reported to have said, "We've made a lot of progress on pasta and things like that—but tofu has been hard for us." We think Bill should try this recipe; it is delicious and still very sloppy!

Moving on to our more eclectic fare, we begin with one of our favorite recipes, Veggie Tacos with Spicy Curry Sauce (p. 153). If you like Indian food and Southwestern cuisine, you'll love these spicy, curried tacos. Another curry favorite is Stuffed Roti with Potato Curry (p. 154) from the Caribbean. Roti is usually eaten with the fingers and with dipping sauces, so it's very messy but lots of fun. We were in a roti shop in Trinidad, West Indies, and they offered a choice of twelve fillings. So, you are only limited by your imagination. A much more elegant curry entree is Bombay Curried Eggs Stuffed in Crepes (p. 156). The use of crepes is a nice break from rice. Fresh ginger, toasted coconut, golden raisins, and chile all blend together harmoniously in this dish.

If you enjoy the smoky, hot flavors of chipotle chiles, then this quick lunch or dinner specialty, Snappy Sautéed Portobello Chipotle Sandwich (p. 158), is a must. While we suggest that you serve it on the Green Chile Focaccia Bread from Chapter 8, it is also good on a big crusty roll when you need to do something a little quicker.

Because portobello mushrooms are so popular now, we have included a dynamic entree called Grilled Portobello Mushrooms and Chipotle Chile Sauce with Peppered Fettucine (p. 160). Chipotle chile is the best chile we have found that blends well with the taste of the mushrooms.

Hot Stuffed Pita Pockets with Harissa Sauce (p. 162) is fast to prepare, and it offers a much more exciting flair to a meal than just a sandwich, with its tangy flavors full of cumin, coriander, and North African chile paste.

Having people over for dinner? Tell them you'll be serving our Marvelous Meatless Spicy Paella (p. 164); it's healthy and elegant, and we'd even bet they'll remember to bring a nice bottle of wine!

If you don't have a tart pan, we suggest you go out and buy one. Most tarts are relatively easy to produce, but they look as though you've been slaving for hours. Our Summer Smart Tart (p. 159) is no exception to this rule, and it is an excellent brunch selection.

Our next five dishes feature a North of the Border flair. Our friend Nancy Gerlach came up with the Vegetable Enchiladas with Chipotle Cream Sauce (p. 166). We suggest that you substitute black beans for the pinto beans in the recipe—an inspiration we attribute to the excellent cuisine of Austin, Texas, which is known for adding black beans to just about everything. The Grilled Corn Potato Cakes with Poblano Chile Lime Vinaigrette (p. 168) is a specialty from the exclusive Boulders Resort in Scottsdale, Arizona. We would be remiss if we didn't admit that this recipe takes a little time, but we promise it is well worth it.

Continuing with our desert favorites, we offer Southwestern Chile-Corn Quiche (p. 170), which has its basis in another popular Southwestern dish, calabacitas, but here we've added a cheese crust and made the filling thicker. Nopalitos, the fleshy oval leaves of the prickly pear cactus, have always been popular in Mexico, and their popularity quickly moved up to the American Southwest. Nippy Nopalitos Huevos Rancheros (p. 172) is quick to prepare and it makes a satisfying brunch or light dinner. We serve Southwest Asparagus Strata (p. 174) year-round because of its taste and convenience. However, we always make it in the spring because we can go down to the irrigation ditches along the Rio Grande and pick the wild asparagus, which has a taste all its own. We even fry this asparagus and make sandwiches with it.

Who doesn't love quesadillas? Grilled Brie Quesadillas with Caribbean Salsa (p. 173) is a guaranteed crowd-pleaser. Feel free to substitute corn tortillas for the flour tortillas if you wish to cut down the fat content even further.

If you just can't seem to get all of the tortillas in your fridge eaten before they are tough enough to crack a tooth, don't despair—Chilaquiles (p. 176) are tailor-made for you! This traditional Mexican casserole calls for stale tortillas as well as lots of other delicious ingredients, such as guajillo chiles, chipotles, garlic, and cheese.

Linguine with Pasilla, Cilantro, and Parsley Pesto

We think it is impossible not to love pesto—especially since we've lowered the fat content in this hot adaptation with a peppery twist. Consider serving it with one of our hot fruit salads from Chapter 3 and your favorite Chardonnay.

24	ounces linguine	¼	cup olive oil
½	cup chopped basil leaves	¼	cup toasted pine nuts
½	cup chopped cilantro leaves	¼	cup grated Parmesan cheese
2	cups chopped Italian parsley	1	tablepoon crushed garlic
1	cup Super-Rich Vegetable Stock (see recipe, p. 4)	2	pasilla chiles, rehydrated, seeds and stems removed, chopped

In a large pot, cook the pasta according to the directions on the package, until the pasta is al dente. Drain the pasta in a colander and place it in a serving bowl.

While the pasta is cooking, in a food processor blend the basil, cilantro, parsley, stock, oil, pine nuts, cheese, garlic, and chiles. Pour over the pasta and toss well. Serve immediately.

Yield: 4 to 6 servings

Heat Scale: Medium

Spicy, Urbane Mac and Cheese

The variety of cheeses in this upscale and tasty dish makes it dangerously delicious! The chiles in the dish as well as the flavored pasta adds a subtle punch and contrasts nicely with the cheeses and the herbs.

1	teaspoon salt
½	cup olive oil
1	pound flavored pasta, such as green or red chile or habanero (see Appendix 2, "Mail-Order Sources")
½	pound mascarpone cheese, softened
1	teaspoon coarsely ground white pepper
½	teaspoon coarsely ground black pepper
4	ounces Gorgonzola cheese, crumbled
½	pound fontina cheese, cut into ¼-inch cubes
¾	cup grated Parmesan cheese
1	habanero chile or 3 serrano chiles, seeds and stem removed, minced
¼	cup minced Italian parsley
2	teaspoons chopped fresh thyme, or 1 teaspoon dried thyme
¾	teaspoon dried oregano
1	teaspoon dried savory
½	teaspoon salt
4	to 5 cups mixed greens, such as Boston or Bibb lettuce, endive, escarole, Mizuna

Bring a large pot of water to a boil, then add the salt and 2 tablespoons olive oil. Add the dry pasta and cook according to the directions on the package. Drain thoroughly and place the pasta in a large bowl lined with paper towels.

Mix the mascarpone, 6 tablespoons oil, and the ground peppers together in a small bowl. Remove the towels from the pasta and stir in the mascarpone mixture. Add the cheeses, chile, parsley, thyme, oregano, savory, and salt and toss the mixture lightly.

Arrange a bed of mixed greens on each plate and mound the pasta-cheese mixture on top. Serve immediately.

Yield: 8 servings

Heat Scale: Medium

Dan Dan Mein (Dan Dan Noodles)

Mary Kinnunen, writing in *Chile Pepper* magazine about Sichuan cuisine, says this dish is definitely yum-yum! Sidewalk snack vendors carried pots of these noodles on shoulder poles (*dan* means "shoulder pole"). Dan Dan noodles became so popular that they began to appear at first-class banquets. Dan Dan Mein, with its strong tastes of spice, is one of Sichuan's most popular foods.

2 cups Super-Rich Vegetable Stock (see recipe, p. 4)

3 tablespoons Pungent Pepper Oil (see recipe, p. 6) or any hot chile oil

1 tablespoon minced garlic

1 tablespoon minced ginger

1 tablespoon vegetable oil

1 tablespoon sesame paste

2 teaspoons sesame oil

1 green onion, chopped

½ pound cooked spaghetti noodles

¼ cup chopped green leaf vegetable, such as spinach or Chinese cabbage

Combine the stock, chile oil, garlic, ginger, vegetable oil, sesame paste, sesame oil, and green onion and heat. Add the noodles and vegetable to the sauce and heat through.

Divide into serving bowls.

Yield: 4 servings

Heat Scale: Hot

Red Hot Lover's Vegetarian Lo Mein

Recipe contributor Darryl Malloy wrote in *Chile Pepper* magazine that every time he makes this dish, his wife is putty in his hands for several days. Needless to say, they eat it often! Heat can be adjusted by increasing or decreasing the amount of chiles. Darryl recommends it very hot.

Sauce:

¼   cup Super-Rich Vegetable Stock (see recipe, p. 4)

1   tablespoon soy sauce

2   cloves garlic, minced

1   tablespoon dry sherry

1   tablespoon hoisin sauce

2   teaspoons sesame oil

1   teaspoon chile paste or hot bean sauce

1   teaspoon minced ginger

¼   teaspoon white pepper

Combine all the ingredients for the sauce.

Lo Mein:

1   pound thin Chinese egg noodles

1   tablespoon peanut oil

2   cloves garlic, minced

3   or 4 Thai chiles or other small, dried Asian chiles

1   medium onion, julienned

¼   cup dry sherry

1   red bell pepper, stem and seeds removed, julienned

1   cup sliced mushrooms

2   carrots, julienned

¼   pound snow pea pods

1½ tablespoons cornstarch mixed with 1½ tablespoons water

2   cups julienned napa cabbage

½   cup chopped green onions

Boil the noodles until done according to directions on the package. Drain and toss lightly with peanut oil to prevent sticking.

Heat a skillet or wok until very hot and add the oil. Stir-fry the garlic, chiles, and onion until the onion is translucent. Add the sherry and reduce for 1 minute.

Add the bell pepper, mushrooms, carrots, and pea pods and stir to coat. Cover for 1 minute, then add the sauce, cover, and continue to cook for 4 minutes. The vegetables should still be crisp. Raise the heat and slowly stir in the cornstarch mixture until the sauce thickens.

Add the noodles and toss to coat. Stir in the cabbage and green onions and serve.

Yield: 4 servings

Heat Scale: Medium

Pod Pourri, Part 5

Hot and spicy retail shops are springing up in malls and strip shopping centers all over the United States. . . . Some industry experts estimate that there are more than 100 shops with names like Some Like It Hot and other variations on the theme. . . . An inmate at the New Mexico Women's Correctional Facility in Grants , New Mexico lost twelve days of good time for possession of "contraband"—four jalapeños hidden in her prison jumpsuit. . . . The world's largest ristra—more than 30 feet long—was draped from the courthouse roof to celebrate the Chile and Cheese Festival on October 2, 1994 in Roswell, New Mexico. . . . A similarly large ristra was fashioned in 1986 by New Mexico State University students—it weighed a half-ton. . . .

Ballistic Baby Bok Choy and Fried Tofu

Because tofu soaks up so many flavors and seasonings, it is ideal to use in many dishes that have a strong flavor base. If you have been eating tofu, consider yourself lucky—it is now touted as a food that reduces some risks of cancer as well as lowering cholesterol levels. If it is used and cooked properly, even your most carnivorous friends can be persuaded to try it. Seduce them with this recipe.

16	ounces firm tofu
3	tablespoons Pungent Pepper Oil (see recipe, p. 6), or 3 tablespoons corn oil and 1 teaspoon crushed, dried santaka or Thai chile or 2 teaspoons New Mexican red chile (see Note below)
1½	pounds baby bok choy, washed and coarsely chopped
4	cloves garlic, minced
6	scallions, sliced
1	red bell pepper, julienned
4	tablespoons water
4	tablespoons soy sauce
2	dried shitake mushrooms, rehydrated and sliced
¾	cup coarsely chopped water chestnuts or jicama
3	teaspoons sugar
2	teaspoons crushed, dried santaka, Thai, or New Mexican red chile
1½	teaspoons cornstarch or arrowroot mixed with 2 tablespoons water
4	cups cooked rice

Cut the tofu into 1-inch slices and place them on paper or linen towels; cover with more towels. Place a cookie sheet on top of the tofu and place several weights (such as canned goods) on top to help squeeze the excess liquid out of the tofu. Drain for 15 to 20 minutes. Cut the tofu into 1-inch cubes.

Heat the oil in a large sauté pan or wok to a medium-high heat. Sauté the tofu cubes, turning them when necessary, to achieve a golden-brown color. Drain the cubes on paper towels and set aside.

In a large skillet with a cover, add the bok choy, garlic, scallions, bell pepper, and water. Cover and steam until the bok choy is tender, about 5 minutes.

Add the soy sauce, tofu, mushrooms, water chestnuts, sugar, crushed red chile, and the cornstarch mixture and toss to mix. Stir lightly until the sauce boils, reduce the heat, and allow it to simmer for 1 minute.

Serve the mixture immediately over hot, cooked rice.

Yield: 4 servings

Heat Scale: Medium to Hot

Note: If you are using santaka or Thai chile, the heat scale will be considerable; if you are using New Mexican crushed red chile, the heat scale will be lower, unless you add more of the crushed chiles.

Spicy Sweet-and-Sour Tempeh

Tempeh is available in health food and whole food stores; not long ago, it was hard to find because it wasn't as mainstream as tofu. Tempeh was originally eaten in Indonesia. The intense flavors of this dish make for a very satisfying entrée. This dish can be served over cooked rice, or it can be served with a crisp salad and some warm pita bread.

1	small fresh pineapple, cleaned		1	teaspoon shoyu
2	tablespoons pineapple juice		1	tablespoon chile-infused oil
2	tablespoons Pungent Pepper Oil (see recipe, p. 6) or any chile-infused oil		8	ounces 5-grain tempeh, cubed
1	tablespoon minced fresh ginger		1	teaspoon sesame oil
3	cloves garlic, minced		2	dried Thai chiles
2	tablespoons minced onion		¼	cup cubed red bell pepper
2	tablespoons rice vinegar		½	cup coarsely chopped onion
½	cup water		1	cup sliced bok choy
¾	cup brown rice syrup		½	cup chopped jicama
3	tablespoons miso		¾	cup bean sprouts
			¼	cup sliced mushrooms

Cut the fresh pineapple into ½-inch cubes and set aside 1½ cups. Puree some of the remaining pineapple in a food processor, drain and measure out 2 tablespoons, and set aside. Refrigerate the remaining fruit.

Heat 1 teaspoon of the oil in a small wok or heavy skillet and sauté the ginger, garlic, and onion for 30 seconds, stirring so the garlic doesn't burn.

Add the remaining oil, vinegar, and water and stir constantly. Add the reserved 2 tablespoons of pineapple juice, the rice syrup, miso, and shoyu and stir until the miso is dissolved. Stir in the cubed pineapple, remove the mixture from the heat, and reserve.

Heat the 1 tablespoon chile oil in a wok or large skillet and sauté the cubed tempeh until it is crisp. Remove it from the wok and drain it on paper towels.

Wipe out the wok with a paper towel. Heat the sesame oil in the wok and quickly sauté the Thai chiles, bell pepper, onion, bok choy, jicama, bean sprouts, and mushrooms until they are heated through but still crisp. Remove the Thai chiles and stir in the reserved tempeh and the pineapple sauce. Heat through and serve immediately.

Yield: 4 servings

Heat Scale: Hot

Terrific Tongue-Tingling Tofu Sloppy Joes

We think of this recipe as a Saturday or Sunday night special. It's fast, easy, and delicious—with very little cleanup. Besides, tofu is good for you. Serve the mixture over good-quality buns.

2	cups firm tofu
2	tablespoons canola oil
¾	cup chopped onion
¼	cup chopped green bell pepper
¼	cup chopped celery
1	(8-ounce) can tomato sauce
1½	teaspoons Worcestershire sauce or tamari sauce
½	teaspoon salt
⅛	teaspoon freshly ground black pepper
1	tablespoon vinegar
¼	cup Three-P Ketchup (see recipe, p. 8) or commercial habanero ketchup (see Note below), or ¼ cup regular ketchup plus ¼ cup chopped green chile, 1 chopped serrano, or 1 chopped jalapeño chile
1	teaspoon sugar
	Toasted buns

Drain the tofu and place on paper or linen towels; cover with more towels. Place a cookie sheet on top of the tofu and place several weights (such as canned goods) on top to help squeeze the excess liquid out of the tofu. Crumble it into a bowl and set aside.

Heat the oil in a medium skillet and lightly sauté the onion, bell pepper, and celery. Add the crumbled tofu and toss lightly.

Add the tomato sauce, Worcestershire sauce, salt, pepper, vinegar, ketchup, and sugar and stir into the tofu. Add a little water if the mixture looks too thick. Reduce the heat, cover, and simmer for 20 minutes.

Serve the mixture on toasted buns.

Yield: 5 to 6 servings

Heat Scale: Medium

Note: Habanero ketchup is available by mail order; see Appendix 2, "Mail-Order Sources."

Veggie Tacos with Spicy Curry Sauce

We've cut out a bunch of the fat from this tasty recipe by substituting corn for the flour tortillas and nonfat yogurt for the sour cream. These tacos are so delicious you'll want to make them a standard item on your dinner menu.

1   tablespoon plus 1 teaspoon safflower oil

1   small onion, chopped

1   shallot, chopped

2   cloves garlic, minced

1   tablespoon curry powder

1   teaspoon ground cumin

½   teaspoon cayenne powder

¼   cup plain nonfat yogurt

1   tablespoon Jalapeño Pepper–Pear Chutney

(see recipe, p. 25) or prepared mango chutney

1   red bell pepper, stemmed, seeded, and julienned

1   yellow bell pepper, stemmed, seeded, and julienned

1   green bell pepper, stemmed, seeded, and chopped

1   purple onion, chopped

12   (4-inch) corn tortillas

In a small skillet, heat 1 teaspoon of the oil and sauté the onions until golden brown. Add the shallot, garlic, curry powder, cumin, and cayenne and sauté for another minute, then remove from the heat. In a bowl, mix together the yogurt, chutney, and the onion mixture and chill in the refrigerator.

In a medium skillet, heat the remaining 1 tablespoon of oil and sauté the bell peppers and onion, until they are soft but still slightly crisp.

Place the tortillas in a tortilla warmer (or between two cloths) and microwave for 25 seconds. Place the sautéed vegetables on a platter and, with the tortillas and curry sauce, allow each person to construct individual tacos or make them all up ahead of time.

Yield: 6 servings

Heat Scale: Medium

Stuffed Roti with Potato Curry

When Nancy Gerlach was visiting the British Virgin Islands, she enjoyed eating this dish at Foxy's Tamarind Bar. Rotis are traditional fare throughout the Caribbean and have been called a West Indian version of a burrito. The bread wrapper is East Indian in origin and always contains something curried.

Dough:

4	cups all-purpose flour	¼	cup plus 2 tablespoons vegetable oil
2	teaspoons baking powder		
1	teaspoon salt		

Sift the flour, baking powder, and salt together in a bowl. Gradually stir in ¼ cup of the oil and enough water to form a ball with the dough. Knead the dough for 5 minutes or until soft. Gather into a ball, cover, and let rise for 15 minutes.

Divide the dough into 4 equal balls. Flatten each and roll out into a circle, 8 to 9 inches in diameter. Heat the remaining 2 tablespoons of oil in a skillet until very hot (a drop of water will sizzle). Reduce the heat and cook rotis for 2 to 3 minutes, until browned, then turn and brown. Remove and cover with a towel until ready to serve.

Filling:

2	cloves garlic, minced	½	teaspoon ground cloves
1	tablespoon minced ginger	½	teaspoon ground black pepper
1	Scotch bonnet or habanero chile or 2 fresh cayenne chiles, stem and seeds removed, minced	¼	teaspoon salt
		3	cups cooked, peeled, diced potato
1	to 2 tablespoons vegetable oil	2	cups water
1	onion, diced	2	tablespoons tamarind paste dissolved in ¼ cup water (optional)
3	tablespoons imported curry powder	1	(15-ounce) can chickpeas (garbanzo beans), drained
1	teaspoon dried thyme		

Sauté the garlic, ginger, and chile in the oil for a couple of minutes. Add the onions and spices and sauté until the onions are soft. Add the potato, water, tamarind, and chickpeas and simmer for 15 minutes, until soft but not mushy.

To serve, place about 1 cup of the filling in the center of a roti. Fold over the sides and fold up the ends, as you would with a burrito. Serve accompanied with the Jalapeño Pepper–Pear Chutney (p. 25) and a hot sauce.

Yield: 4 servings

Heat Scale: Medium

Bombay Curried Eggs Stuffed in Crepes

The curried eggs make an unusual and exotic filling for crepes; serve them for brunch or dinner. Once the crepes and the sauce are made, it is a simple matter to put the two together and present an entree that is elegant and easy—and it's ecstasy on the taste buds.

Crepes:

4	eggs, or 2 eggs plus ½ cup egg substitute	2¼	cups low-fat milk
¼	teaspoon salt	4	tablespoons melted butter
2	cups all-purpose flour		

Combine the eggs and salt. Gradually add the flour and the milk, beating the mixture with a whisk. Beat in 2 tablespoons of the melted butter. Refrigerate the mixture for 1 hour.

Heat a small sauté pan and, using a brush, coat the bottom and sides with a thin coat of the remaining 2 tablespoons of melted butter.

Remove the mixture from the refrigerator, whisk it briskly, and pour about ¼ cup of the mixture to the sauté pan, swirling it to coat the bottom of the pan. Allow it to cook for 30 seconds, then flip it over with a spatula and cook another 30 seconds. Remove the cooked crepe to a plate and cover with a sheet of waxed paper. Repeat this process until all the batter is used. Reserve 12 to 14 crepes for this recipe; wrap and freeze the remainder for future use.

Filling:

2	tablespoons butter
2	tablespoons olive oil
1½	teaspoons curry powder (preferably Spice Islands)
1	teaspoon freshly grated ginger
¼	teaspoon salt
1	clove garlic, minced
½	cup minced onion
⅛	teaspoon freshly grated lemon zest
½	cup golden raisins or currants
¾	cup chopped apple
1	teaspoon (or more) of your favorite habanero hot sauce, or
1	teaspoon freshly chopped habanero chile
3	tablespoons chopped chutney (preferably Major Grey's mango chutney)
3	tablespoons flour
1	cup Super-Rich Vegetable Stock (see recipe, p. 4)
1	cup light cream
5	hard-boiled eggs, shelled and diced
¼	cup toasted coconut

Preheat the oven to 325 degrees. Melt the butter and add the olive oil in a medium skillet. Add the curry powder, ginger, salt, garlic, onion, lemon zest, raisins, apple, hot sauce, and chutney and sauté over low heat for 2 minutes, stirring occasionally.

Sprinkle the flour and stir it into the mixture. Add the stock and light cream, whisking and then stirring the mixture as it thickens. Stir in the diced eggs.

To assemble, fill the crepes with the egg mixture. Place the crepes in an oiled glass cooking dish, and bake for 10 minutes. Sprinkle the crepes with the toasted coconut and serve immediately.

Yield: 6 to 7 servings

Heat Scale: Medium

Note: This recipe requires advance preparation.

Snappy Sautéed Portobello Chipotle Sandwich

This is the perfect meatless alternative for game day. It offers interesting textures, lots of heat, and best of all is served on Melissa's Green Chile Focaccia Bread from Chapter 8.

2 tablespoons margarine	1 loaf Green Chile Focaccia Bread (see recipe, p. 213), in 8 thick slices
2 pounds portobello mush-rooms, brushed and sliced	
1 large onion, cut into thin rings	Balsamic vinegar
3 chipotle chiles in adobo sauce, stems removed, chopped	

Place the margarine in a large sauté pan over medium-high heat. Add the mushrooms, onion, and chipotles and sauté until the onions are caramelized. Remove the mixture from the heat and divide equally among four slices, then give each a splash of the vinegar. Top each half with another slice of the bread and serve.

Yield: 4 servings

Heat Scale: Medium Hot

Summer Smart Tart

While we like this tart for brunches in summertime, it is just as nice in the winter or fall. Simply accompany the tart with seasonal side dishes and a little apple cider, and you're ready to go.

1	prepared pie crust	1	tablespoon capers, rinsed and drained
2	cups reduced-fat mozzarella cheese, grated	1	tablespoon olive oil
6	roma tomatoes, sliced	1	tablespoon fresh basil, minced
4	cloves garlic, minced		
½	cup black olives, rinsed		
2	New Mexico green chiles, roasted, peeled, stems and seeds removed, chopped		

Bake the pie crust according to the directions on the package until it is barely done, not browned, then remove it from the oven and cool to room temperature. Spread the cheese evenly on the bottom of the crust. Place the tomatoes on top of the cheese, overlapping each slice over the next in a concentric circle.

Preheat the oven to 350 degrees. In a bowl, combine the garlic, olives, chiles, capers, oil, and basil, then spread the mixture over the tomatoes. Place the tart in the oven for about 15 minutes, or until the cheese is melted, the tomatoes have softened, and the crust has browned. Cool to room temperature.

Yield: 6 servings

Heat Scale: Medium

Grilled Portobello Mushrooms and Chipotle Chile Sauce with Peppered Fettucine

Somehow, having a grilled portobello mushroom seems to satisfy even the most carnivorous diner. Eating this mushroom is akin to eating a steak, and it can take on a multitude of seasonings and flavors. In this recipe, the sauce has more ingredients than the main course! Serve this elegant dish with a light, crunchy salad from Chapter 3.

4 large, fresh portobello mushrooms	¼ cup freshly grated pecorino or Parmesan cheese
¼ cup red wine vinegar	½ teaspoon imported curry powder
2 cloves garlic, minced	¼ teaspoon freshly ground black pepper
2 tablespoons olive oil	
1 cup safflower oil	2 chipotle chiles in adobo sauce
⅓ cup fresh lemon juice	¼ teaspoon salt
¼ cup tahini (sesame paste)	12 ounces fettucine pasta
2 teaspoons soy sauce	1 tablespoon olive oil
1 tablespoon Worcestershire sauce	½ teaspoon freshly ground black pepper
1 tablespoon whole-grain mustard	

Clean the mushrooms and place them in a shallow glass pan. Mix the vinegar, garlic, and olive oil together and pour the mixture over the mushrooms, then turn the mushrooms to coat. Cover tightly and marinate for 1 hour at room temperature.

While the mushrooms are marinating, make the sauce: Combine the safflower oil, lemon juice, tahini, soy sauce, Worcestershire sauce, mustard, cheese, curry powder, black pepper, chipotle chiles, and salt in a blender and blend until smooth, about 30 seconds. Allow the mixture to sit at room temperature while the mushrooms are being grilled.

Cook the pasta according to the directions on the package. Drain the pasta thoroughly, return it to the pot, add the olive oil and black pepper, toss, and keep warm.

Remove the mushrooms from the marinade and grill for 2 to 3 minutes on each side, or sauté them in a heavy skillet.

Divide the pasta on 4 warmed dinner plates, place a grilled mushroom on top of the pasta, and top each mushroom with the sauce. Serve immediately.

Yield: 4 servings

Heat Scale: Mild

Note: This recipe requires advance preparation.

The Meatless Way

"I have no doubt that it is part of the destiny of the human race, in its gradual improvement, to leave off eating animals, as surely as the savage tribes have left off eating each other when they came in contact with each other."

Henry David Thoreau

"My hearse will be followed not by mourning coaches but by herds of oxen, sheep, swine, flocks of poultry, and a small aquarium of live fish, all wearing white scarves in honor of the man who perished rather than eat his fellow creatures."

George Bernard Shaw

"A vegetarian is a person who won't eat anything that can have children."

David Brenner

Hot Stuffed Pita Pockets with Harissa Sauce

From Ellen Burr of Truro, Massachusetts comes this great main dish. She confesses: "In the '60s I became an addicted chilehead after sniffing a vat of Tabasco in Louisiana. Ever since, I've brought home the perfect, and eminently edible, memento: hot peppers, canned, bottled, dried and powdered, including harissa, which I discovered not in a souk but in a Santa Fe market! Here is a family favorite, my healthy version of falafel, low in fat and high in flavor."

1 small onion, sliced	¼ cup prepared tahini or hummus
1 small red bell pepper, stem and seeds removed, sliced	Salt
1 large clove garlic, minced	4 whole wheat pita rounds, halved and warmed
1 tablespoon olive oil	8 lettuce leaves
¼ teaspoon ground cumin	1 tomato, sliced
¼ teaspoon ground coriander	1 small cucumber, peeled and thinly sliced
1 (19-ounce) can cannellini beans, rinsed and drained	8 sprigs cilantro or parsley
1 teaspoon prepared harissa	

Sauté the onion, bell pepper, and garlic in the oil for a couple of minutes. Add the cumin and coriander and cook for an additional 5 minutes.

 Stir in the beans, harissa, and tahini. Mash the beans slightly and heat over a low heat until hot. Salt to taste.

Line the pita pockets with lettuce, tomato, and cucumber. Stuff with the hot bean mixture and cilantro sprigs.

Serve warm or cold, with extra harissa on the side.

Yield: 4 servings

Heat Scale: Mild

Note: Harissa is a North African chile paste. If none is available, substitute 5 dried red New Mexican chiles, rehydrated, and puree with a clove of garlic and ½ teaspoon each ground cumin, cinnamon, coriander, and caraway.

Marvelous Meatless Spicy Paella

There's no reason why people should miss out on the Spanish treat of paella just because they don't eat meat. We admit that this recipe does have a lot of ingredients, but it's really worth the trouble!

3¼	cups Super-Rich Vegetable Stock (see recipe, p. 4)		2	shallots, minced
¼	teaspoon saffron threads		1	small onion, minced
1	head of garlic, broken into cloves, unpeeled		2	serrano or jalapeño chiles, seeds and stems removed, minced
2	yellow bell peppers, seeded and cut into bite-size strips		3	roma tomatoes, diced
1	red bell pepper, seeded and cut into bite-size strips		1	tablespoon fresh oregano, minced
1	orange bell pepper, seeded and cut into bite-size pieces		1	tablespoon fresh thyme, minced
2	small zucchini, trimmed and cut into rounds		1½	cups medium-grain white rice
2	tablespoons extra-virgin olive oil		2	lemons, quartered
			2	tablespoons chopped fresh parsley

Combine the stock and saffron in a medium saucepan and bring the mixture to a rapid boil. Reduce the heat and simmer, covered, for 25 minutes. Set aside.

In another saucepan, place the garlic in enough water to cover, then boil for 5 minutes or until tender. When done, drain the water and let the garlic cool. When the garlic can be handled comfortably, peel the cloves and set aside.

Preheat the oven to 400 degrees. Place the garlic, bell peppers, and zucchini in a rectangular baking dish. Pour 3 tablespoons of the stock and 1 tablespoon of the olive oil on top of the vegetables. Bake for 30 minutes or until the vegetables are tender, stirring twice during baking. When done, set aside.

In a deep skillet, heat the remaining 1 tablespoon of olive oil over medium heat. Add the shallots, onion, and serranos and sauté until the onions are brown. Add the tomatoes, oregano, and thyme and cook for about 4 minutes, or until the liquid has evaporated. Add the rice and the remaining vegetable stock and bring to a boil. Simmer, covered, for 20 to 30 minutes, or until the rice is tender. Gently fold in the roasted vegetables and simmer, covered, for 5 more minutes. Transfer the paella to a colorful serving dish and garnish with the lemon wedges and parsley. Serve with crusty rolls.

Yield: 4 servings

Heat Scale: Medium

The Origins of Vegetarianism

"It was in 1838 that vegetarianism may be said to have had its beginning in the United States, since that was the year in which an American Health Convention endorsed vegetable diets; but America would have to wait until after the Civil War to achieve the formal organization of vegetarianism, which had been consecrated in England as early as 1809; it was in 1813 that Percy Bysshe Shelley took time out from composing such sensual verse as *Ode to the West Wind* in order to demonstrate, with a more commendable sense of duty, that the human body is designed to deal with vegetable foods and vegetable foods only (he had perhaps neglected to examine the evidence to the contrary provided by human dentition)."

Waverly Root and Richard de Rochemont

Vegetable Enchiladas with Chipotle Cream Sauce

From Nancy Gerlach, these enchiladas are about the tastiest meatless enchiladas imaginable. Rice can be substituted for or combined with the pinto beans, or you could also use black beans and corn.

Sauce:

2	chipotle chiles in adobo sauce, stems removed	1¼	cups heavy cream
4	canned tomatillos, drained	1½	teaspoons sugar
		¼	teaspoon ground cinnamon

Place the chiles and tomatillos in a blender or food processor and puree until smooth. Combine with the cream, sugar, and cinnamon in a saucepan and simmer until thickened, about 10 minutes.

Enchiladas:

1	cup chopped onion	1½	teaspoons oregano
2	cloves garlic, chopped	¼	teaspoon ground cumin
1	to 2 tablespoons vegetable oil	½	cup cooked pinto beans
1	medium potato, diced, boiled, and drained	1	cup grated longhorn cheese
1	zucchini, diced	8	corn tortillas
1	cup chopped mushrooms		Cilantro leaves
4	green New Mexican chiles, roasted, peeled, stems and seeds removed, diced		

Sauté the onion and garlic in the oil until soft. Add the potato and zucchini and continue to cook until the potato is browned and the zucchini is done but still crisp. Add the mushrooms, chiles, oregano, and cumin and sauté until the mushrooms are soft, about 5 minutes. Remove and stir in the beans and cheese.

To assemble, wrap the tortillas in plastic and microwave on high for 10 seconds. Fill the tortillas with the vegetables and roll. Heat in an oven at 350 degrees until the cheese melts, about 10 minutes. Top with the sauce, garnish with cilantro and serve.

Yield: 4 servings

Heat Scale: Mild

Grilled Corn Potato Cakes with Poblano Chile Lime Vinaigrette

From chefs Charles Wiley and Jeff Gustie of the Boulders Resort in Scottsdale, Arizona, this recipe is delicious enough to grace any chilehead's table.

Grilled Corn Potato Cakes:

1   small purple onion, diced
1   tablespoon margarine
3   russet potatoes
1   ear sweet corn, grilled until slightly blackened, kernels removed from cob

¼   cup plain nonfat yogurt
2   teaspoons ground ancho chile or ground New Mexican or other pure chile powder
    Kosher salt and freshly ground pepper to taste

Sauté the onion in the margarine until the onions have browned slightly.

Steam or boil the potatoes for 25 to 30 minutes with skins on. Peel while still warm and mash coarsely in a mixing bowl. Add the onion, corn, yogurt, chile powder, salt, and pepper and mix well. Spread this mixture ¾-inch thick on an 8×8-inch baking pan. Cool in the refrigerator, then, using a 2-inch circular cutter, cut out 12 cakes.

Poblano Chile Lime Vinaigrette

6   poblano chiles, roasted, peeled, stems and seeds removed
½   cup white wine
¼   cup vegetable oil
2   tablespoons chopped fresh cilantro
4   cloves garlic

2   shallots
2   teaspoons Dijon mustard
2   limes, juiced
    Kosher salt and freshly ground black pepper
    Cilantro sprigs

Place all the ingredients in a blender and process until smooth. This recipe makes approximately 1½ cups.

To assemble, divide the vinaigrette equally among 4 plates (the vinaigrette should cover the bottom of each plate). On each plate, stand three corn cakes on edge and garnish with cilantro sprigs.

Yield: 4 servings

Heat Scale: Mild

Southwestern Chile-Corn Quiche

The interesting cheese crust with minced chiles sets the scene for the filling of this Southwestern-style quiche. Serve it with one of the salads from Chapter 3 and a decadent dessert from Chapter 9.

2	cups fine cheese-cracker crumbs	⅛	teaspoon freshly ground white pepper
3	tablespoons melted butter	1¼	cups low-fat milk
3	tablespoons canola oil	2	beaten eggs
1	serrano chile, seeds and stem removed, minced	¾	cup diced New Mexican green chiles
½	cup minced onion	1	cup diced zucchini
2	tablespoons flour	2	cups cooked fresh corn, or 1 (17-ounce) can whole corn, drained
½	teaspoon salt		
⅛	teaspoon celery seed		

Mix the 1½ cups of crumbs with 2 tablespoons of the melted butter, 2 tablespoons of the canola oil, and the serrano chile. Set aside ½ cup of the crumbs for the topping. Press the remaining crumbs into a 9-inch glass pie pan, making a smooth, firmly packed shell.

Preheat the oven to 400 degrees.

In a small saucepan, add the remaining 1 tablespoon melted butter, the remaining 1 tablespoon canola oil, and onion and sauté for 30 seconds. Sprinkle the flour over the onion, add the salt, celery seed, and pepper, and stir over a low heat until blended, about 20 to 30 seconds. Add the milk, all at once, and stir it with a wire whisk constantly until the mixture starts to thicken.

Add ¼ cup of the milk mixture to the beaten eggs and whisk. In a steady, slow drizzle, add the milk-egg mixture back to the mixture in the saucepan, whisking constantly. Remove the mixture from the heat.

Stir in the green chiles, zucchini, and corn and slowly and carefully pour this mixture into the prepared pie shell. Sprinkle the top with the reserved cheese crumbs.

Bake for 15 to 20 minutes. Remove the quiche from the oven and allow it to stand for 5 minutes.

Cut the quiche into 6 pieces and serve.

Yield: 6 servings

Heat Scale: Medium

Nippy Nopalitos Huevos Rancheros

Outside of the Southwest, the cactus is thought of as a nuisance to be avoided; however, in the Southwest it is a symbol of the desert and a source of food. In early spring, the young pads of the prickly pear cactus are harvested, despined, and used in many dishes. The taste is pleasant—similar to green beans. The cactus pads, called nopalitos, are available in Latin markets and by mail order. For the salsa, use a recipe from Chapter 1 or your favorite purchased salsa.

6	(8-inch) flour tortillas	1	cup chopped New Mexican green chile
2½	cups shredded sharp cheddar cheese	12	eggs, poached or fried
1	(16-ounce) jar nopalitos, rinsed and drained	1½	cups salsa, at room temperature
2	cups chopped tomatoes		

Preheat the oven to 350 degrees. Place the tortillas directly on the oven rack and heat them for 3 to 5 minutes. Remove them from the oven and place them on cookie sheets.

Sprinkle the cheese, nopalitos, tomatoes, and green chile over the tortillas. Bake in the oven until the cheese just starts to melt. Top each tortilla with 2 warm eggs, spoon the salsa on top, and serve immediately.

Yield: 6 servings

Heat Scale: Medium (depending on the heat scale of the green chile and the salsa)

Grilled Brie Quesadillas with Caribbean Salsa

These South of the Border grilled cheese sandwiches can be made with either corn or flour tortillas. According to Nancy Gerlach, in Mexico they are often made with uncooked corn tortillas that are filled and then fried, but it is easier to use cooked ones. Cheese is the traditional filling, but almost anything will work. Instead of folding them over as in this recipe, you can also layer the tortillas with the filling, cook, and then cut the stack like a pie.

1½	cup finely diced pineapple	1	teaspoon grated ginger
3	tomatillos, husks removed, finely diced	2	tablespoons vegetable oil
½	to 1 habanero chile, stem and seeds removed, finely diced, or substitute ground habanero	4	(8-inch) flour tortillas
		8	ounces Brie cheese, rinds removed, cut in wide strips, or 8 ounces goat cheese, crumbled
2	tablespoons chopped fresh cilantro		

To make the Caribbean salsa, combine the pineapple, tomatillos, chile, cilantro, and ginger and toss them with 2 teaspoons of the oil.

Prepare the barbecue grill.

Soften the tortillas, if necessary. Place one-quarter of the cheese on half of each tortilla. Top with the salsa and fold the tortilla in half.

Brush the top of the quesadillas with a little of the remaining oil and place them on the grill, oiled side down. Cook for a minute, brush the top with oil, then turn and cook for an additional minute.

Cut each quesadilla in thirds, arrange on a plate, and serve.

Variation: Quesadillas can be heated on an ungreased heavy skillet. Heat until brown spots appear, turn, and heat on the other side until the cheese has melted.

Yield: 4 servings

Heat Scale: Hot

Southwest Asparagus Strata

Serve this great entree when asparagus is at its height. This recipe has variations all over the place! Basically, strata is an egg- and bread-based dish that is enhanced with vegetables, spices, or herbs. The classic mix is 6 eggs to 3½ cups of milk; you can cut down the mix to 4 eggs, 2 egg whites (or egg substitute), and use low-fat milk. Use a full-bodied bread—nothing wimpy. Buy day-old French bread from a good bakery.

1	pound day-old French bread, cut into 1½-inch cubes	2	tablespoons butter
3½	cups low-fat milk	½	pound button mushrooms, sliced
6	eggs, or 4 whole eggs and 2 egg whites, or use egg substitute for part of the egg mixture	½	cup minced sweet onion
		1	cup chopped New Mexican green chile, excess water blotted out
½	teaspoon freshly ground white pepper	2	teaspoons chopped fresh chives
½	teaspoon salt	2½	cups shredded Jarlsberg, Gruyère, or Swiss cheese
1	pound fresh asparagus, cleaned and sliced into 2-inch pieces	2	tablespoons grated Parmesan cheese

Arrange the bread cubes on a cookie sheet, toast 4 inches under the broiler, stirring and checking the cubes until they are a golden-brown. Take care not to burn the cubes. Place the cubes in a large bowl.

Beat the milk, eggs, pepper, and salt together and pour 1½ cups of the beaten mixture over the bread cubes. Toss the cubes occasionally to coat them thoroughly. Set aside the remaining milk-egg mixture.

Steam the asparagus for 3 minutes, then rinse in cold water, drain, and set aside.

Melt the butter in a skillet and sauté the mushrooms and onion until the onion wilts. Remove the mixture from the pan with a slotted spoon, allowing any liquid to drain off, and place in a small bowl. Add the green chile and chives to the mushroom mixture and toss.

Lightly grease a shallow 3- or 4-quart ovenproof casserole or a 9×13×2-inch pan. Layer one-third of the soaked bread cubes in the bottom of the pan. Top this mixture with half of the asparagus, half of the mushroom–green chile mixture, and sprinkle with half of the cheeses. Repeat the next layer with half of the remaining bread cubes, asparagus, mushroom-chile mixture, and the remaining cheese. Top with the remaining bread cubes and pour the reserved milk and egg mixture over the top.

The strata can be baked right away in an oven at 325 degrees for 45 minutes; cover the top with aluminum foil if it starts to brown too quickly. Or, the casserole can be covered and refrigerated overnight. To bake the next day, allow the casserole to stand at room temperature for 20 minutes, then bake in an oven at 325 degrees for 60 to 70 minutes.

Yield: 6 to 8 servings

Heat Scale: Mild

Chilaquiles

In Mexico, no tortilla is ever thrown away, even if it is stale. *Chilaquiles*, or "broken-up sombrero," makes use of stale corn tortillas and any leftovers, such as chicken or chile sauce. Reputed to cure a *crudo*, or hangover, this is one of Nancy Gerlach's favorite breakfast/brunch dishes, and it's a great way to eat a bowl of chile sauce.

6   dried guajillo or New Mexican chiles, stems and seeds removed

2   chipotle chiles in adobo sauce, including 1 tablespoon of the sauce

1   large onion, chopped

2   cloves garlic, chopped

1   tablespoon vegetable oil

1   large tomato, peeled and seeds removed, chopped

¼   teaspoon cumin seeds

1   cup Super-Rich Vegetable Stock (see recipe, p. 4)
Vegetable oil

6   stale tortillas, cut in strips

8   ounces queso fresco, crumbled, or grated Monterey Jack cheese

1   small onion, sliced very thin and separated into rings

Preheat the oven to 350 degrees.

Cover the guajillo chiles with hot water and let them sit for 15 to 20 minutes or until softened. Drain and place them in a blender or food processor along with the chipotles and the sauce, and puree until smooth, adding a little water if necessary.

Sauté the onion and garlic in the 1 tablespoon of vegetable oil until they are soft. Stir in the pureed chile sauce, tomato, and cumin and simmer for 10 minutes. Put the sauce in a blender or food processor and puree until smooth. Strain for a smoother sauce. Return the sauce to the pan, add the stock, and simmer for 15 minutes.

Pour the vegetable oil in a pan to the depth of 2 inches and heat to 365 degrees. Fry the tortilla strips in the oil until they are chewy but not crisp. Drain well.

To assemble, place a layer of the tortillas on the bottom of a serving dish. Cover with a layer of cheese and then the sauce. Repeat several times.

Bake in the oven for 15 minutes or until hot. Garnish with additional grated cheese and onion, then serve.

Yield: 4 to 6 servings

Heat Scale: Medium

Alternative Medicine Quite Peppery

In a special report in *USA Today* (January 1, 1995), entitled
"Can Alternative Medicine Help?" experts Jim Duke, Ph.D.,
and Deepak Chopra, M.D., were asked to comment on the
effect of alternative medicine on certain ailments. Their com-
ments make them sound like chileheads.

- Back Trouble: "Try biting into a hot pepper when the pain
  is most excruciating. Peppers are almost as inexpensive
  as aspirin."

  Duke

- Asthma: "An attack might be alleviated by an early
  Mexican Maya mixture, [which is] hot chocolate with
  hot pepper."

  Duke

- Weight Control: "Favor spicy foods with astringent,
  pungent, and bitter tastes, like bitter greens, horseradish,
  garlic, fenugreek, curry, onions, and jalapeño peppers,
  which increase the metabolism."

  Chopra

- Arthritis: "When pain or stress builds, I have a cup of
  cayenne-ginger tea. I believe more in hot pepper's ability
  to desensitize pain and ginger's anti-inflammatory com-
  pounds than in anything OK'd by the FDA lately."

  Duke

Vital Vegetables

Ever since nutritionists have been begging us to eat more vegetables, there has been a concerted effort to be more creative with them, even making a sturdy vegetable dish the centerpiece of the meal. Grocery stores have also gotten into the act; there are far more different kinds of vegetables available than ever before. We have even noticed that when new items are introduced, there are little tear-off cards explaining exactly what kind of vegetable it is, offering nutritional information and suggestions for cooking and serving—smart and helpful.

We have included many different types of vegetables in this chapter, with the additional twist of making them mild, medium, and hot—utilizing the chiles in every way imaginable. Some of the mild recipes are good foils for the blazing entrees of Chapter 6, as they incorporate some milk or cream for a soothing, but slightly tangy, sauce. Tiffany's Tangy Spinach (p. 183) is one such recipe; it is practically a tradition in New Mexico. You can tell how long a person has lived in New Mexico if he or she asks, "What's Tiffany's Restaurant?"—you know that person has lived here fewer than twenty years, because that's when the restaurant that used to be in Cerrillos burned down.

Artichoke Hearts Au Gratin (p. 184) has no historical value, just gastronomical. It's smooth and mildly spiced, and it's an elegant side dish to serve at a buffet, brunch, or dinner. However, be aware that the food you eat after the artichoke can sometimes taste sweet. Artichokes have a substance called cynarin that causes this effect. There is an Italian artichoke aperitif called Cynar, which is hard to find in the U.S.; if you can find it, try it, because it is so unique and tasty. We first sampled it in Florence, Italy.

The next vegetable dishes have an international theme, as they are from our globe-trotting friends. Finadini Birenhenas (p. 185) is an eggplant dish from Guam that is lively with jalapeños and then tempered with rich coconut milk. If you have never tried the clay pot method of roasting vegetables, you will be in for a treat when you make Spicy Moroccan Clay Pot Vegetables (p. 186). Paprika, red chiles, and fresh ginger heat up this dish, and when it is done, a sprinkling of fresh mint adds an exotic touch. From Poland we present Polish Baked Stuffed Mushrooms (p. 188); the stuffing is rich with shallots, hot paprika, and feta cheese. Since these are so rich, we suggest serving them with one of the lighter entrees. Another real Polish favorite is Polish-Style Sauerkraut (p. 189). The unusual combination of ingredients is sure to please even the pickiest sauerkraut eater! The hot paprika jazzes up the taste buds, while the mushrooms, raisins, and juniper berries add a depth of flavor.

Moving on to China and India, we have some wonderful treats in store, starting with Fried Eggplant in Chile Sauce (p. 190) from the Sichuan province of China. The dish incorporates the traditional tastes of salty, sweet, sour, and spicy, and some of these tastes come from pickled chiles and fresh ginger. "Korean" Carrots (p. 191) is a recipe from Siberia, the Russian Far East, brought to that area by the Koreans who settled there. Serving this dish at room temperature will intensify the cayenne chile flavor. It is a simple recipe to prepare, but it's exotic in taste.

Three recipes from India round out the gastronomical world tour of vegetables. Shajahanni Aloo, Almond-Spiced Potatoes (p. 192), is one example of how Indian cooks have embellished and embraced the New World vegetable, the potato. This delicious dish is rich with yogurt, almond butter, and red chiles. The unusual ingredients to entice your taste buds are cardamom and saffron. One note about saffron: a little bit goes a long way, and that is a good thing, because it is the world's most expensive spice. Do not overpower a recipe with more saffron than the recipe calls for, because that will only adulterate the taste.

Cauliflower is one of the most popular vegetables in India, especially in northern India. There must be at least a hundred ways to prepare it! One of these recipes, Aloo Goby, Spiced Cauliflower (p. 193), shows the versatility of this vegetable dish with red chiles, tomatoes, yogurt, and cardamom. The interesting touch comes from the heavy cream that is poured over the finished dish. It is very rich, so serve it with one of the lighter entrees.

A lighter Indian vegetable side dish is Saibhaji, East Indian Sautéed Vegetables (p. 194), which combines a few vegetables, a few spices, and tastes like a million bucks. We think it is actually a dish created to use leftover vegetables!

A transitional recipe, Green Chile Latke (p. 195), is from Israel via Albuquerque, New Mexico; this recipe combines the best of both worlds, so to speak. Even if you don't celebrate Hanukkah, you should make these delicious latkes; they are not complicated and are truly a different taste treat served with applesauce or sour cream. Choose a light entree, something that will complement the flavors of the latke.

The next group of recipes are from the U.S.A. with strong influences of Asia and Asian ingredients. Brave Braised Veggies with Garlic, Chile, and Red Curry (p. 196) contains both red and green chile, a real boon for chile lovers. This vegetable melange really tempts the taste buds with green beans (or long beans), bell peppers, and bok choy. Look for baby bok choy in some of the specialty stores; it is especially delicious. The next vegetable medley is

Grilled Teriyaki Vegetables (p. 197), combining zucchini, onions, tomatoes, and mushrooms with a spicy teriyaki marinade. The slow grilling enhances the flavor of the vegetables. A transitional recipe that has Asian overtones is Luscious Lettuce Rolls (p. 198); instead of the traditional eggroll wrapping, this recipe uses blanched lettuce leaves. The stuffing is spicy, with a dash of Italian cheese. We call it a multinational dish!

The next set of recipes features a single type of vegetable as the star. Beatific Beets (p. 199) really do live up to their heavenly name. Very small beets, combined with raspberry vinegar and hot sauce, will accent any meal. Besides, our yoga instructor said beets are good for your liver! A New World vegetable around since about 5500 B.C.—the squash—gets a modern treatment in Blistering Baked Squash with Bombastic Blueberries (p. 200). Acorn squash is baked with apples, habanero chiles, and blueberries. The habanero chile goes well with fruit dishes as well as some vegetables, because it has slightly fruity overtones. Sweet and Sour and Spicy Eggplant (p. 201) has slightly smoky overtones with the addition of chipotle chiles in adobo sauce. Chipotles are smoked jalapeños, and they add a real depth of flavor to any dish, not only vegetables. We also use chipotle champagne vinegar in this recipe, which adds a dash of taste without the tartness of other vinegars.

Spicy Summer Grilled Corn (p. 202) features corn, with bell peppers, chiles, currants, and cloves as co-stars. Grilled corn has a different, unique taste, and it is well worth the effort; frozen, thawed corn can be substituted, but the taste will be sorely lacking in this recipe. In the recipe Dilly Beans (p. 203), fresh green beans are marinated with carrots, garlic, chiles, and dill and make a refreshing addition to any summer meal. Serve it with a lunch or a brunch and watch your guests come back for more. It can be served chilled or at room temperature.

Tiffany's Tangy Spinach

This recipe is legendary here in New Mexico; it is from the old Tiffany's Restaurant in Cerrillos that burned down many years ago. It is spicy, creamy, and, best of all, easy to make. Serve it with one of the main dishes from Chapter 6.

1	(16-ounce) box frozen spinach	½	teaspoon Lawry's seasoned salt
1	serrano chile, stem and seeds removed, minced	½	teaspoon fines herbes
½	cup low-fat sour cream	2	teaspoons drained, grated prepared horseradish

Cook the spinach according to the directions on the package. Drain the spinach thoroughly and keep it warm.

Mix together the chile, sour cream, seasoned salt, fines herbes, and horseradish in a small bowl. Stir the mixture into the warm spinach and heat slowly over a low temperature until the entire mixture is hot. Be careful not to use too high a temperature, or the sour cream will break down. Serve immediately.

Yield: 4 servings

Heat Scale: Mild

Vegetable Facts

- The most popular vegetables, according to the FDA, are, in order: potatoes, iceberg lettuce, tomatoes, onions, carrots, celery, corn, broccoli, green cabbage, and cucumbers.
- The annual vegetable consumption in the United States in 1995 was 102 pounds, up from 81 pounds ten years before.
- Ten percent of U.S. adults do not eat fruits or vegetables in a given day.

Artichoke Hearts Au Gratin

Artichokes never tasted as good as they do in this dish. It is easy to make and elegant to serve. We suggest serving it on a bed of mixed greens, either fresh or sautéed.

2	(14-ounce) cans water-packed artichoke hearts	¼	teaspoon freshly ground white pepper
3	tablespoons butter	⅓	cup sifted all-purpose flour
1	tablespoon oil	1½	cups milk
1	clove garlic, minced	1	egg, slightly beaten
3	serrano or jalapeño chiles, seeds and stems removed, cut into rings	½	cup grated Swiss cheese
		2	tablespoons finely crushed breadcrumbs
½	teaspoon salt		

Preheat oven to 450 degrees. Rinse the artichoke hearts and drain on paper towels. Cut them into thin slices.

Heat the butter and oil in a skillet, then add the artichokes, garlic, and chiles and sauté over a low heat for 2 minutes, tossing lightly. Remove the artichoke mixture to a shallow pan with a slotted spoon, allowing the butter to drip back into the skillet.

Stir the salt, pepper, and flour into the remaining butter and simmer for 30 seconds. Add the milk, whisking constantly. Simmer over a low heat, whisking, until the mixture thickens. Remove from the heat.

Slowly whisk into the milk the beaten egg mixture, then add ¼ cup of the cheese and blend until smooth. Pour over the artichokes and sprinkle with the remaining cheese and the breadcrumbs.

Bake in the oven, uncovered, for 15 minutes.

Yield: 6 servings

Heat Scale: Mild

Finadini Birenhenas

We thank Janet Go for this recipe; she wrote about Guam in *Chile Pepper* magazine. This recipe turns eggplant into a hot and spicy accompaniment. We think it would make an exotic sandwich spread!

4	small Japanese eggplants with stems
1	medium onion, chopped
2	lemons, juiced
2	fresh hot chiles, such as jalapeños, stems and seeds removed, minced
1	teaspoon salt
½	cup coconut milk

Prick the eggplants and, while holding them by the stem, cook directly over flame until soft (the eggplant will be blackened on the outside). Soak in cold water to cool and peel.

Combine the onion, lemon juice, chiles, and salt and mix. Holding the eggplant by the stem, cut it and mash it into the mixture. Add the coconut milk, mix, and serve.

Yield: 4 servings

Heat Scale: Medium

Veggie Web Site

Now, cyber-vegetarians have their own control central on the Internet. Called "Veggies Unite," the Web site designed by Indiana University features an extensive recipe collection, veggie events, links to other meatless sites, and an extensive collection of articles on health, medicine, and nutrition. Reach Veggies Unite at:

http://www.honors.indiana.edu/~veggie/recipes.cgi.

Spicy Moroccan Clay Pot Vegetables

What really perks up this dish is the judicious use of chiles, the roasting technique, and a liberal sprinkling of freshly chopped mint. Invest in a clay roasting dish; it is wonderful to use year-round, and it is especially useful in the cold months when you can't use an outdoor grill. This vegetable dish is a spicy and hearty one, so serve it with one of the lighter main dishes from Chapter 6.

2	tablespoons grapeseed oil or olive oil	½	teaspoon salt
1	cup diced sweet onion (preferably Vidalia)	¾	cup Super-Rich Vegetable Stock (see recipe, p. 4)
1	teaspoon paprika	10	whole, peeled garlic cloves
2	teaspoons crushed red chiles or pure red chile powder	4	carrots, peeled and cut into 2-inch pieces
1	teaspoon grated fresh ginger	2	cups broccoli florets
¼	teaspoon ground whole cumin seeds	3	cups potatoes, peeled and cut into 1½-inch cubes
¼	teaspoon freshly ground white pepper	½	cup freshly chopped mint

If you are using a clay pot, immerse it in water according to manufacturer's directions (usually 30 minutes).

Preheat the oven to 350 degrees; if you are using a clay pot, do not preheat the oven.

Heat the oil in a small sauté pan, add the onion, and sauté for 1 minute. Add the paprika, chile, ginger, cumin, pepper, salt, and stock and bring to a boil. Remove the mixture from the heat and set aside.

Place the garlic, carrots, broccoli, and potatoes in the clay cooker (or any small, covered ovenproof container). Pour the stock mixture over the vegetables. Cover the vegetables and roast for 30 to 45 minutes, checking to see when the vegetables are cooked through.

When the vegetables are done, arrange them on a heated platter and sprinkle them with the fresh mint.

Yield: 6 servings

Heat Scale: Mild to Medium (depending on the heat of the crushed red chile)

Pod Pourri, Part 6: Texas Stuff

Governor Bush of Texas has signed legislation making the jalapeño the official pepper of Texas. . . . What are you waiting for, habanero-haven California?. . . . A demographics magazine suggested in 1993 that a part of Texas be separated and the new state be named Jalapeño. . . . An editorial in the *Albuquerque Journal* pontificated: "So, let the state of Texas make all the claims it wants about its chile prowess. New Mexicans know better, and take the Texas bragging with several grains of salt around the rims of their margaritas—the perfect accompaniment to a plate of green chile enchiladas, extra hot."

Polish Baked Stuffed Mushrooms

This recipe is from Sharon Hudgins, who wrote about Poland in *Chile Pepper* magazine. She says: "Mushroom-picking is a national pastime in Poland, and mushrooms are an important ingredient in many Polish dishes. In the mountainous region of the south, mushrooms are often combined with locally made cheeses, as in the following recipe. The Poles would use fresh *Boletus edulis* mushrooms and salty sheep's milk cheese known as *bryndza*—but large *champignons* and Greek feta are an acceptable substitute outside of Poland."

16	large fresh *Boletus edulis* mushrooms or 16 large *champignons* (about 1 pound)	1	tablespoon finely chopped fresh parsley
6	tablespoons melted butter or margarine, divided in two parts	1	teaspoon mild or medium-hot paprika or to taste
1	shallot, finely chopped	½	cup dry breadcrumbs
1	large clove garlic, finely chopped	½	cup finely crumbled sheep cheese, such as feta

Preheat the oven to 350 degrees.

Carefully twist the stems off the mushrooms, leaving the cap whole. Finely chop the mushroom stems.

Heat half of the butter, add the mushroom stems, shallot, and garlic, and sauté for about 5 minutes. Remove the pan from the heat and stir in the parsley, paprika, and breadcrumbs. Add the crumbled cheese and mix well.

Lightly brush the outside of each mushroom cap with the remaining butter. Stuff each mushroom cap with a heaping tablespoon of the filling, shaping the filling by hand into a small dome. Use all of the filling to stuff the 16 mushroom caps. Arrange the mushrooms, filling side up, in a lightly oiled baking dish. Bake for 15 to 20 minutes.

Serve hot as a first course or as an accompaniment to broiled steaks or chops.

Yield: 4 servings as an appetizer, 6 to 8 servings as an accompaniment

Heat Scale: Mild

Polish-Style Sauerkraut

Thanks to Sharon Hudgins again for this recipe, and she says it's a Polish favorite. Pickled vegetables, such as cucumbers, cauliflower, and peppers, are a staple of the Polish diet. Sauerkraut, or pickled cabbage, is a year-round favorite and is used as an ingredient in many dishes or is served as an accompaniment to braised or roasted meats. If you've never cared for the taste of sauerkraut, the following recipe is certain to change your mind!

¼	cup vegetable oil	⅓	cup raisins or chopped prunes
1	very large onion, chopped	1	cup chicken stock
1½	teaspoons hot paprika	½	cup medium-dry or sweet white wine
2	(2-pound) cans sauerkraut, drained and rinsed	6	whole juniper berries
½	cup chopped dried mushrooms, such as *Boletus edulis* or porcini	2	whole cloves
		1	bay leaf

Heat the oil, add the onion, and sauté until the onions turn golden. Reduce the heat to low, sprinkle the paprika over the onions, and cook, stirring constantly, for 30 seconds. Immediately stir in the sauerkraut and the remaining ingredients and mix well.

Bring the mixture to a boil, reduce the heat, and cover the pan. Simmer, stirring occasionally, for 1 hour.

Yield: 6 servings

Heat Scale: Mild

Fried Eggplant in Chile Sauce

This recipe is from Mary Kinnunen, who investigated the chile pepper cuisine of Sichuan province in the People's Republic of China. This dish has the mixed tastes of salty, sweet, sour, and spicy.

4	cups peanut oil	1	green onion, chopped
3½	cups fresh eggplant, peeled and cut into cubes 2 inches long, 1 inch wide, and ¾-inch thick	⅓	cup Super-Rich Vegetable Stock (see recipe, p. 4)
		1	tablespoon soy sauce
		1	tablespoon vinegar
4	tablespoons chopped pickled chile, jalapeño suggested	1	tablespoon sugar
		1	teaspoon cooking wine
1	tablespoon minced ginger	1	teaspoon cornstarch dissolved in 2 tablespoons warm water
1	tablespoon minced garlic		

Heat the oil in a wok to 375 degrees. Add the eggplant and deep-fry until soft, about 3 minutes. Remove, drain, and keep warm. Pour off all but 1 tablespoon of the oil.

Add the chile and stir-fry until the oil becomes red. Add the ginger, garlic, and onion and stir-fry until fragrant, about 1 minute. Add the stock, eggplant, soy sauce, vinegar, sugar, and cooking wine and stir-fry for 2 minutes.

Stir in the cornstarch paste and simmer to thicken the sauce. Serve with rice.

Yield: 4 servings

Heat Scale: Medium

"Korean" Carrots

We thank *Chile Pepper*'s contributing editor Sharon Hudgins, who wrote about Siberia. This appetizer recipe is from the Russian Far East, and it is referred to as "Korean" Carrots because the recipe was brought to this region of Russia by the Koreans who now live there. In the markets in Vladivostok, this spicy carrot dish is sold in clear plastic tubes as a snack food or convenience food. But it also makes a nice—and deceptively spicy— addition to any buffet table.

1	pound carrots, peeled and finely shredded	½	teaspoon salt
1½	to 2 teaspoons cayenne powder	3	tablespoons soybean or other vegetable oil

Put the carrots into a bowl and press them with a wooden spoon or masher until they begin to release some of their juice. Make a well in the center of the carrots, all the way to the bottom of the bowl. Add cayenne and salt into the well.

Heat the oil until very hot, pour over the cayenne, and stir to mix the oil and spices. Then stir to mix the pepper-oil with the carrots.

Let sit at room temperature for 30 minutes. Serve at room temperature. If you want the flavor to be even hotter, make the appetizer a day in advance, refrigerate, and then let sit for 30 minutes at room temperature before serving.

Yield: 6 servings as an appetizer

Heat Scale: Medium

Shajahanni Aloo (Almond-Spiced Potatoes)

Richard Sterling gave us this recipe, and he continues his around-the-world quest of The Great Spice Bazaar, as reported in *Chile Pepper* magazine. Potatoes are one of many New World crops now common in India: chiles, tomatoes, peanuts, and okra are also popular. This recipe calls for almond or cashew butter (simple finely crushed nuts), which you can buy or make easily with a food processor or mortar and pestle. Be sure to peel the almonds first.

½   cup vegetable oil

1   pound potatoes, peeled and sliced

1½   cups plain yogurt

2   teaspoons ground red chile, such as hot New Mexican

3   tablespoons almond butter or cashew butter

4   yellow onions, peeled and sliced into rings

1   tablespoon cardamom powder
Few strands saffron, or
1 teaspoon ground turmeric

½   cup water
Salt

3   tablespoons heavy cream
Chopped fresh cilantro
Small dried red chiles

Heat half the oil and fry the potatoes in batches until brown. Remove the potatoes and drain any remaining oil from the pan.

Add the remaining oil. Combine the yogurt, chile, and nut butter. Add to the pan and cook, stirring often, until the oil rises to the top. Add the onion rings and cook until soft.

Return the potatoes to pan along with the cardamom, saffron, water, and salt to taste. Mix well and cook, shaking the pan now and then, for 20 minutes. The oil should be floating on the top.

Pour the cream over the top and serve garnished with chopped cilantro and dried red chiles.

Yield: 4 to 6 servings

Heat Scale: Medium

Aloo Goby (Spiced Cauliflower)

This is another recipe from Richard Sterling on his pilgrimage to northern India. Cauliflower is one of the most popular vegetables in India. In the northern part of the country, it's downright inescapable. Fortunately, no two cooks seem to prepare it quite the same way. Consider this recipe not as a formula, but as a point of departure.

2 teaspoons vegetable oil	½ pound tomatoes, peeled, seeds removed, coarsely chopped
2 teaspoons sugar	1 cup plain yogurt
1 large cauliflower, divided into florets	2 teaspoons ground cardamom
2 onions, sliced and fried	Chopped fresh cilantro
2 teaspoons crushed red chile, such as New Mexican	Salt
	¼ cup heavy cream

Heat the oil to low, add the sugar, and brown, stirring constantly. Add the cauliflower and mix well to coat with the caramel. Stir in the onions, chile, tomatoes, and yogurt and cook, covered, over low heat until the cauliflower is tender. Stir in the cardamom and cilantro and cook an additional 5 minutes. Add salt to taste.

Pour the cream over the top and serve.

Yield: 4 to 6 servings

Heat Scale: Medium

Saibhaji
(East Indian Sautéed Vegetables)

This dish is one that could accompany any East Indian feast. It is quick and easy; make it ahead and just keep it warm. It could also be served with any of the entrees. It is a truly a versatile vegetable dish.

3	tablespoons oil	2	tomatoes, coarsely chopped
½	cup chopped onions	2	jalapeño or serrano chiles, seeds and stems removed, finely minced
1	clove garlic		
1	teaspoon finely minced fresh ginger	¾	cup leftover cooked carrots, potatoes, peas, or green squash (optional)
½	teaspoon ground cumin		
1	teaspoon ground coriander seeds		
3	bunches spinach, cleaned and stems removed		

Heat the oil in a large sauté pan. Sauté the onions for a few minutes, then add the garlic, ginger, cumin, and coriander. Add the spinach and stir. Add the tomatoes and chiles and cook until the spinach is tender. Add any leftover you choose. Many cooks often mash the mixture before it is served. Serve hot.

Yield: 5 servings

Heat Scale: Medium

Green Chile Latke

This recipe is from Tommy Hudson, president of Village Inns of Albuquerque. Tommy says, "My wife Karen is Jewish and fond of the latke that are served at big gatherings during Hanukkah. Since I work for a pancake house, it seems natural for me to make these potato pancakes. You can cook these ahead of time and reheat them in the oven. Surprisingly, they don't lose a bit of taste this way; in fact, I think they're better. These can be served plain or with applesauce or sour cream."

4   medium potatoes, peeled and shredded
3   eggs
1   teaspoon chopped garlic
4   green New Mexican chiles, roasted, peeled, stems and seeds removed, chopped
¼   cup finely chopped onions
    Salt
    Olive oil

Combine potatoes, eggs, garlic, chiles, onion, and salt in a bowl. It should have the consistency of pancake batter. Cover and chill, in the refrigerator, for 30 minutes.

Coat a pan with oil, preferably an electric skillet to keep the temperature between 375 and 385 degrees. Mix the batter and spoon it onto the pan. Cook about 3 minutes, or until golden brown, then flip over and repeat. Drain on paper towels.

Yield: 4 servings

Heat Scale: Mild

Brave Braised Veggies with Garlic, Chile, and Red Curry

We thank Mark Berlin for this recipe. He explored Asian markets for *Chile Pepper* magazine. The recipe combines green Thai chiles with red curry paste. As Mark says, "Red and green. Some people see STOP! But chile lovers see GO FOR IT!"

2 purple onions, cut in wedges

2 tablespoons chile oil

6 cloves garlic

2 cups long beans or green beans, cut in 4-inch pieces

1 red bell pepper, stem and seeds removed, julienned

1 green bell pepper, stem and seeds removed, julienned

1 medium bunch bok choy, cut diagonally in ½-inch pieces

6 green Thai chiles, minced, or 4 large jalapeño chiles, stems and seeds removed, chopped

2 tablespoons red curry paste

2 tablespoons Szechuan Garlic Chili Sauce

1 cup Super-Rich Vegetable Stock (see recipe, p. 4)

In a wok or large heavy pan, sauté the onions in the chile oil until they are translucent. Stir in the garlic, beans, and bell peppers and stir-fry for 3 minutes, stirring occasionally.

Add the bok choy, chiles, curry paste, Szechuan Sauce, and stock and simmer until the paste dissolves and the sauce thickens slightly.

Yield: 6 servings

Heat Scale: Hot

Grilled Teriyaki Vegetables

The vegetables suggested in this recipe can be replaced with some of your own personal favorites. Whenever you are grilling, you need to pay attention—don't let the vegetables burn! Serve this dish with your favorite entrée and summer salad.

½ cup olive oil

½ cup teriyaki marinade

2 cloves garlic, minced

2 teaspoons pure red chile powder, such as Chimayo

3 small zucchini, cut into 1-inch slices

2 onions, peeled and cut into quarters

8 cherry tomatoes

3 medium crookneck squash, cut into 1-inch cubes

8 large button mushrooms

Whisk the olive oil, marinade, garlic, and red chile together in a large bowl.

Add the zucchini, onions, tomatoes, squash, and mushrooms and toss to coat the vegetables. Marinate at room temperature for 30 minutes.

Thread the vegetables on metal skewers, alternating the different types. Place the skewers on the grill over medium hot coals. Grill for about 15 minutes, basting frequently with the marinade and turning often.

Yield: 6 servings

Heat Scale: Mild

How Squash Got Its Name

"Did early man squash this vegetable before eating? No. Does it look as if it's been squashed? No. The word 'squash' is another example of how many Indian words the colonists changed because they had trouble pronouncing them. The Narragansett word for squash was *askatasquash*, meaning 'something eaten green.' This word referred specifically to summer squash."

Don Voorhees

Luscious Lettuce Rolls

Almost any type of cooked vegetable can be used as a filling for this versatile side dish. Swiss chard can be substituted for the Boston lettuce. They can be prepared ahead and then quickly sautéed.

1 slice coarse white bread, crust removed	¼ cup New Mexican green chile, diced
½ cup milk	3 tablespoons grated Pecorino Romano cheese or Parmesan cheese
6 large leaves Boston lettuce or Swiss chard	
1 egg yolk	½ teaspoon salt
1 cup blanched broccoli florets, finely chopped	¼ teaspoon freshly ground black pepper
1 cup blanched finely diced carrots or golden beets	2 tablespoons olive oil

Soak the bread in the milk for 10 minutes, then drain it, squeeze it dry, and set aside.

Bring a large saucepan of salted water to a boil, add the lettuce leaves for 5 seconds, remove immediately, and place them in a large bowl of ice water. Drain the leaves thoroughly on paper towels, patting off excess water.

Beat the egg yolk in a medium bowl and add the drained bread, broccoli, carrots, chile, cheese, salt, and pepper and mix thoroughly.

Spoon a line of filling across the middle of each leaf, then fold the sides of the leaf over the ends of the filling. Starting from the stem end, roll up each leaf tightly, to completely enclose the filling.

Heat the oil in a large skillet, add the rolls (seam side down), cover, and sauté for 5 minutes over a low heat, turning once. Serve immediately.

Yield: 6 servings

Heat Scale: Mild

Beatific Beets

There are now so many varieties of beets available in grocery stores and specialty whole food stores that we would be remiss if we didn't give the beet some credit as a terrific vegetable. Buy the smallest beets you can find; they will be the most tender. And if you can't buy them, grow them (see Appendix 2, "Mail-Order Sources").

1	pound fresh, small beets, cooked, peeled, cut into ¼-inch slices	1	tablespoon commercial hot sauce of choice
1	cup chopped red onion	¼	teaspoon salt
⅓	cup olive oil	¼	teaspoon freshly ground black pepper
¼	cup raspberry vinegar		

Put the beets into a small ceramic bowl, then add the onion, oil, vinegar, hot sauce, salt, and pepper and lightly toss.

Cover and refrigerate for 4 hours or overnight, to allow the flavors to meld.

Allow the mixture to reach room temperature before serving, and then toss again.

Yield: 4 to 6 servings

Heat Scale: Medium

Note: This recipe requires advance preparation.

Blistering Baked Squash with Bombastic Blueberries

In this recipe, we combine not only a vegetable but also a fruit and a few well-chosen chiles. Serve it when blueberries are in season, although frozen blueberries will work as well, with a little flavor loss.

4	acorn squashes, cut in half lengthwise, seeds removed
4	tablespoons butter
2	tablespoons canola oil
1	cup finely chopped apple
1	fresh habanero chile, seeds and stem removed, finely minced, or 1 teaspoon habanero powder

⅓ cup firmly packed brown sugar

12 ounces fresh blueberries or frozen blueberries, thawed and drained

Preheat the oven to 375 degrees.

Place the cut squash in a shallow baking pan (or pans) and pour ½ cup water into each pan. Cover tightly with aluminum foil and bake for 30 minutes.

Heat the butter and oil in a small skillet and sauté the apple, habanero chile, brown sugar, and blueberries over low heat for 1 minute.

Remove the squash from the oven and make several slices in the squash, taking care not to cut through the skin. Divide the apple mixture and add an equal amount to each squash, pressing into the slits. Cover tightly and bake for 15 minutes.

Remove the foil and bake, uncovered, for an additional 15 to 20 minutes.

Yield: 8 servings

Heat Scale: Medium (hotter if you add more habaneros)

Sweet and Sour and Spicy Eggplant

If you have been using cheap wine vinegars, throw them out! They will ruin your food. The chipotles in this recipe add a bit of smokiness to the dish. This dish goes well with a spicy curry entree, cooled with a side of yogurt and cucumbers.

3   to 4 tablespoons olive oil
1   cup diced onion
2   small eggplants, unpeeled and diced into ½-inch cubes
2   chipotle chiles in adobo sauce, chopped
1   bay leaf
¼   cup raisins, softened in water for 20 minutes and drained

⅓   cup chipotle champagne vinegar or red wine vinegar
¾   cup water
¾   cup chopped tomatoes, drained
½   teaspoon salt
¼   teaspoon freshly ground black pepper

Heat the oil in a large skillet, add the onion and the eggplant, and sauté for 12 minutes, stirring occasionally. Add the chiles, bay leaf, raisins, and vinegar, cover, and simmer for 8 minutes, or until the vinegar has evaporated. Stir in the water, cover, and simmer for 20 minutes, or until most of the water has evaporated. The eggplant should be just slightly moist.

Remove the skillet from the heat, discard the bay leaf, and stir in the tomatoes, salt, and pepper. Serve immediately.

Yield: 6 servings
Heat Scale: Medium to Hot

Spicy Summer Grilled Corn

We like to serve this delicious vegetable relish in the summer, when fresh corn is at its peak. We also grow (and buy) fresh corn, parboil it briefly, drain thoroughly, and freeze it for future use. This recipe goes well with any of the main dishes in Chapter 6.

5 ears sweet corn, shucked and grilled, or 4 cups frozen corn, thawed	1 clove garlic, minced
3 tablespoons corn or canola oil	1 cup natural cider vinegar
½ cup diced red bell pepper	1 cup water
½ cup diced green bell pepper	⅓ cup dry currants
1 cup minced sweet onion, such as Vidalia	¼ cup granulated sugar
2 serrano chiles, stems and seeds removed, minced	2 whole cloves, ground in a spice blender, or ¼ teaspoon ground cloves
2 jalapeño chiles, stems and seeds removed, minced	½ teaspoon salt
	½ teaspoon whole mustard seed

Grill the corn until it is almost done. Allow it to cool and then cut the kernels off the cob and set aside.

Heat the oil in a medium saucepan, add the bell peppers, onion, chiles, and garlic, and sauté for 45 seconds, or until the onion is softened. Add the reserved grilled corn and sauté for 1 minute.

Add the vinegar, water, currants, sugar, cloves, salt, and mustard seed and bring the mixture to a boil. Allow the mixture to boil for 30 seconds, then reduce the heat, partially cover, and simmer for 20 minutes.

The mixture can be served warm or chilled.

Yield: 5 servings

Heat Scale: Medium

Dilly Beans

Connie Galvin of Eckert, Colorado says that her mother has been canning Dilly Beans for years. Connie has adapted her recipe to simply marinate the beans for a quick and fancy addition to any antipasto platter.

½ pound fresh green beans, stems removed	1 head fresh dill, or 2 teaspoons dill seed
1 carrot, peeled and cut in ¼-inch slices	1 cup distilled white vinegar
3 whole cloves garlic	1 cup pickled jalapeño liquid or water
2 fresh chiles, such as cayenne or jalapeños, julienned, or 2 teaspoons crushed red chile	1 teaspoon salt

Blanch the beans and carrots for 2 minutes in boiling water, then drain. Rinse with cold water until cool enough to handle. Pack the beans, carrots, garlic, chiles, and dill in a sterilized quart jar.

Bring the vinegar, jalapeño liquid, and salt to a boil. Pour over vegetables to cover.

Refrigerate for 24 hours before serving.

Yield: 1 quart

Heat Scale: Medium to Hot

Note: This recipe requires advance preparation.

Vegetable Cooking Basics

"All vegetables, whether they are steam-cooked or not, should be done as quickly as possible, and in as little water. In this way at least 50 percent of the minerals are collected in the water. They should be drained at once, and either prepared for serving or allowed to cool in the icebox and another day. If they are to be used later, they should be underdone rather than tender, since the reheating will cook them again; and of course they should not be seasoned and buttered until they are ready to be used, except for the herbs you may have cooked with them. Vegetables cooked for salads should always be on the crisp side, like those trays of zucchini and slender green beans and cauliflowerlets in every *trattoria* in Venice, in the days when the Italians could cook correctly."

M. F. K. Fisher

Bold Breads

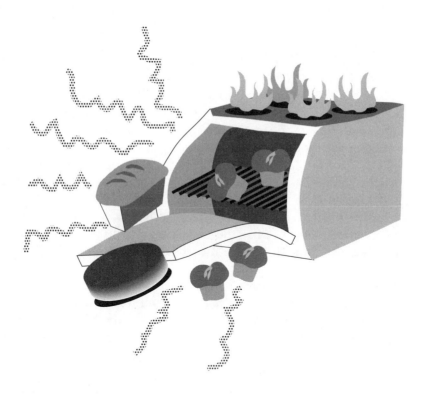

As Emily Post professed, "Bread is like dresses, hats, and shoes—in other words, essential!" The bountiful breads in this chapter are indeed essential, at least to the connoisseur of chiles. We've included our favorite recipes that are fruity and fiery as well as those that are hearty and heated. Bread is one of those universally accepted foods; there are few cultures on earth that do not rely on bread for daily sustenance.

With that thought in mind, we begin our chapter with a double dose of chile madness. The Two-Pepper Biscuits (p. 209) feature both jalapños and black pepper as well as the calorie-saving low-fat buttermilk. Try these with your favorite chile-spiked jam!

The next several recipes have an international flair. Bolillos (p. 210), a type of roll, is a traditional Mexican favorite. They can be filled with a combination of tomatoes, sprouts, avocados, lettuce, and strips of New Mexican green chile; they are also delicious when they are stuffed with grilled vegetables and dressed with some oil and vinegar. Serve this versatile roll with soups or salads. Hot Chile Tortillas (p. 211) is another Mexican favorite, as well as being popular in the American Southwest. In Mexico, they are frequently cooked on a *comal*, a type of Mexican griddle. Interesting ingredients abound in Mofo Sakay, Hot Bread (p. 212), a bread from Madagascar. The bread is fried to a light golden-brown, which brings out the flavors of curry powder, ginger, and watercress.

A little olive oil and our Green Chile Focaccia Bread (p. 213) are all you need to make a magnificent Italian meal. We suggest you pair this bread with the Pasilla, Cilantro, and Parsley Pesto in Chapter 6 or even the Thai Pesto in Chapter 1.

Our next five selections combine fruits and squash with chiles to create extraordinary dessert or breakfast breads. The Lemon Chutney Serrano Bread (p. 214) offers an East Indian accent that is characterized by being both smooth and hot. This bread is also good when accompanied by a slice of your favorite cheese.

Dried cherries are the stars of our Dried Cherry Ancho Orange Muffins (p. 215). The cherry is said to date as far back as 300 B.C. and was named after the Turkish town of Cerasus. While fresh cherries are available from May through August, you can enjoy this recipe year-round with the dried version.

Even to the non-squash lover, zucchini bread is almost always enjoyed. Our Pasilla Carrot Zucchini Bread (p. 216) is some of the moistest bread you'll ever taste. Remember that bigger is not always better when picking out a zucchini; those in the 4-inch to 6-inch range are the best tasting.

Melissa has successfully killed more blackberry bushes than probably anyone else alive. Although she cannot seem to get one to grow in her backyard, she still loves them dearly. Our Cultured Blackberry Cornbread (p. 217) offers a lot of zing (due to the use of red chile) as well as the sweet taste of summer.

You know how truly low-fat dishes often seem as though something is missing? We promise that while our Heavenly Green Chile Pineapple Banana Bread (p. 218) is one of the best bets in this chapter in terms of keeping calories and fat grams low, it is also really good!

What's that crunchy stuff on your salad? Why, Red Chile Croutons (p. 219), of course. While this recipe calls for cubed sourdough bread, you might also like to use the Green Chile Focaccia Bread (p. 213) for a twice-as-nice sizzling salad bite.

Red Chile Twists (p. 220) are the perfect accompaniment to soups, stews, and salads, as well as being a delicious appetizer. Try using different types of chile powder for a variety of flavored twists.

The next bread section is a bit cheesy—tasting that is! The No Bake Habanero Ricotta Cheese Hearts (p. 221) are a completely nontraditional bread that your guests will surely love. It's full of flavor and heat; however, the habanero can be substituted if you'd like to tame things down a bit.

Cheese and chile play a major role in the next recipe, Habanero Cheese Straws (p. 222). This traditional Southern favorite is typically made with cayenne, but we like the extra kick from the habanero. Cheddar-Charged Chile Biscuits (p. 223) combine Southern-style biscuits with Southwest chile. Have a warm biscuit for breakfast—that way, you'll get some protein and a charge of vitamin C from the chile. The next recipe, Chile Cheese Puffs (p. 224), is quite rich and tastes like heaven. The presentation of the whole circle of the baked puffs is quite impressive, even though they are so very easy to make.

And don't forget the Green Chile and Goat Cheese Muffins (p. 225). While they are a great addition to many meals, they are especially nice with Southwestern food, such as the Vegetable Enchiladas with Chipotle Cream Sauce in Chapter 6.

Another muffin recipe, Jazzy Carrot Ancho Muffins (p. 226), is a tasty combination of ancho chile, honey, carrots, walnuts, and sesame seeds. Since these freeze well, make a double batch so you'll always have some around for a snack or for breakfast. For those of you with a sweet tooth, spread the muffins with red chile honey or jalapeño jelly.

The last four recipes are yeast-based and take a little more time than the other quick breads, but they are well worth the effort. Sweet Potato–Cayenne Dinner Rolls (p. 227) is an unusual recipe with its roots in the South. Think of these rolls as a delicious way to get some vitamins C and A. Pasilla chiles and molasses add a unique flavor to Positively Pungent Pasilla Bread (p. 228). Even though the bread needs two risings, you can do other things in the meantime (for example, reading this cookbook!). Quick Chipotle Casserole Bread (p. 230) is the fastest of the yeast bread recipes. The addition of the chipotle gives the bread a faint smoky taste, and it would add a nice accent to an interesting salad or soup. We like to make the next recipe, Seriously Serrano Dill Bread (p. 231) in the summer, when we can snip fresh dill and pick fresh serranos from the garden. For a decadent treat, try spreading the warm slices with softened butter or cream cheese mixed with dill.

Given the variety of breads in this chapter, there is truly something for everyone. Some are low in fat, some are richer; others abound with cheese and chile, while some combine chile and fruit. We have included some breads with international backgrounds, and all the recipes are unique. Bread may be an essential part of life, but it sure doesn't have to be boring!

Two-Pepper Biscuits

As a native Tarheel, F. Wayne Morris of Wilimington, North Carolina grew up with pickled or fresh hot peppers on the table at almost every meal. He contributed the following simple recipe, which he came up with a couple of years back. According to Wayne, his immediate family loves it and even his 83-year-old father, who basically will not eat anything that is "different," likes these two-pepper biscuits.

2   cups self-rising flour
2   to 3 fresh jalapeño chiles,
    stems and seeds removed,
    finely chopped
½   teaspoon freshly ground
    black pepper

2   tablespoons grated Parmesan
    or Romano cheese
1   to 2 tablespoons vegetable
    shortening (not oil)
1   cup low-fat buttermilk

Preheat the oven to 425 degrees.

Combine the flour, jalapeños, black pepper, and cheese in a large mixing bowl and mix well, using a fork. Cut the shortening into the flour with a fork or pastry cutter. Make a well in the flour and add the buttermilk, a little at a time, stirring, until all the flour is incorporated into a fairly stiff dough.

Place the dough on a floured board, sprinkle with additional flour, and knead into a ball. Roll out the dough to ½-inch to ¾-inch thick. Cut out 3-inch biscuits and place, slightly touching, on an ungreased baking sheet.

Bake for 15 to 18 minutes or until golden-brown.

Variation: Use other fresh chiles or, in a pinch, rinsed pickled chiles. You can also add fresh chopped herbs such as thyme, rosemary, or oregano.

Yield: 12 to 14 biscuits

Heat Scale: Mild

Bolillos

We thank Mark Preston for this traditional Mexican recipe. Even though bolillos are nonpungent, they are an essential element for a great Mexican torta or sandwich.

1½ cups boiling water	1 package dry yeast
¼ cup vegetable shortening	¼ cup warm water
2¼ tablespoons sugar	5 cups all-purpose flour
1½ teaspoons salt	

Combine the boiling water, shortening, 2 tablespoons of the sugar, and salt in a large mixing bowl and stir to dissolve.

In a small bowl, mix the yeast, warm water, and the remaining ¼ tablespoon sugar and allow the mixture to sit for 5 minutes. Stir this mixture into the shortening mixture.

Add 2½ cups of the flour to the shortening mixture and beat it for a minute. Cover the mixture and let it rise in a warm place until the batter rises and begins to bubble.

Stir in the remaining 2½ cups of flour until the batter becomes a stiff ball. Knead the dough on a lightly floured board until it is smooth and elastic, adding more flour if needed. Place the dough in a greased bowl and allow it to rise for 1 hour, or until it has doubled in size.

Turn the dough out on a lightly floured board, punch it down, and let it stand for 5 minutes. Divide the dough into 8 equal pieces, roll the pieces with your hand, taper the ends, and flatten slightly. Put each onto a greased cookie sheet, cover, and allow the rolls to double in size, about 30 to 45 minutes.

Preheat the oven to 375 degrees. Bake the rolls for 20 minutes, or until they are golden-brown. Cool them on a wire rack.

Yield: 8 rolls

Heat Scale: Mild

Hot Chile Tortillas

We thank Nanette Blanchard for this recipe. The tortillas are delicious and spicy and can be served alone, stuffed with cheese and rolled, or used as a wrapper for you favorite filling.

3 cups unbleached flour	½ cup butter or vegetable shortening
½ teaspoon salt	
2 teaspoons dried ground piquin chiles	1 cup warm water

Mix the flour, salt, chiles, and butter in a food processor bowl or a bread machine on the Manual setting. Slowly add the warm water until the mixture forms a smooth, moist ball.

Remove the dough, divide it into 12 equal balls, cover with plastic wrap, and let the dough rest for 30 minutes in a warm place.

Flatten each ball in a tortilla press or with a rolling pin to the desired thickness, usually about ⅛ inch.

Cook each tortilla on a preheated, hot griddle on medium heat. Turn the tortilla every 10 seconds for about 1 minute. As it cooks, it will develop some puffing and some dark spots. Place each cooked tortilla under a terry cloth or linen towel. Place the tortillas in a plastic bag and store in the refrigerator until they are needed.

Yield: 12 tortillas

Heat Scale: Medium

Pod Pourri, Part 7: College Chile Antics

In Athens, Ohio, at Ohio University, male students are conducting Saturday Night with the Boys Habanero Eating Contests. . . . Meanwhile, the Alpha Kappa Alpha Sorority at the University of North Texas was suspended from group activities and five of its members have been convicted of hazing, a misdemeanor, because "pledges were struck with paddles and forced to eat hot peppers". . . .

Mofo Sakay (Hot Bread)

This interesting hot bread recipe is from Madagascar; it is very spicy and very easy to make. The unusual combination of ingredients is sure to please your palate.

5 red serrano or jalapeño chiles, seeds and stems removed, minced	1 cup minced onion
	3 cloves garlic, minced
2 cups all-purpose flour	2 teaspoons minced fresh ginger
1 tablespoon baking powder	1½ cups minced watercress
1 tablespoon imported curry powder	1½ cups water
1 teaspoon salt	Vegetable oil

Combine all of the ingredients, except the oil, in a large bowl and mix thoroughly. Cover the bowl lightly with a towel and allow the mixture to stand for 1 hour.

Heat the oil in a deep-fryer or a skillet with high sides. Drop the dough by tablespoons into the hot oil without crowding the dough, and fry until the bread is a dark, golden-brown. Remove the bread from the pan, drain on paper towels, and repeat the process until all of the dough is used up. Serve warm.

Yield: About 2 dozen hot bread balls

Heat Scale: Hot

Green Chile Focaccia Bread

Green chile is the perfect addition to this wonderful Italian bread. Perfect for an hors d'oeuvre or with a meal, this recipe is easily doubled or tripled.

2   cups warm water
    (about 110 degrees)

2   envelopes active dry yeast

12 tablespoons olive oil

10 cups unbleached
    all-purpose flour

4   teaspoons salt

½   cup chopped New Mexican
    green chile

2   cups milk

2   teaspoons coarse salt

Place the water in a bowl, then whisk in the yeast and half of the olive oil. In a separate mixing bowl, combine the flour, salt, and green chile. Stir the yeast mixture and milk into the flour mixture with a sturdy spatula, until the flour is well combined, mixing once vigorously. Cover the bowl with plastic wrap and allow the dough to rise until it doubles in size, about 1 hour.

Spread 1½ teaspoons of the remaining oil in two 11×17-inch jelly-roll pans. Turn the dough out of the bowl and divide between the two pans. Pat and press the dough to fill each pan completely.

If there seems to be too much dough, let it rest and continue in a few minutes. Using your pinky finger, poke cavities in the focaccia about every two inches. Drizzle each pan with equal amounts of the remaining oil and sprinkle with the coarse salt.

Allow the dough to rise again, until it doubles in size.

Preheat the oven to 450 degrees and set a rack to the lower third of the oven. Bake the bread for 25 minutes, or until it is a light golden-brown color. Remove from the oven and serve immediately, or cool the pan on a rack for later use. Reheat the bread at 375 degrees for 6 or 7 minutes.

Yield: 2 loaves

Heat Scale: Medium

Lemon Chutney Serrano Bread

Citrus and serranos make wonderful baking partners. This bread works well as a nice jump start to breakfast or as a tasty late-night snack.

2½ cups all-purpose flour
½   cup granulated sugar
½   cup brown sugar
1   tablespoon baking powder
1   tablespoon finely shredded lemon peel
½   teaspoon salt
1   egg, slightly beaten

1¼ cups milk
1   serrano chile, seeds and stem removed, minced
¾   cup chutney, chopped
¼   cup cooking oil
1   tablespoon lemon juice
1   cup chopped pecans

Preheat the oven to 350 degrees. In a large mixing bowl, combine the flour, sugars, baking powder, lemon peel, and salt. In a smaller bowl, combine the egg, milk, serrano, chutney, oil, and lemon juice. Mix the egg mixture into the flour mixture, stirring well. Add the nuts, then transfer the batter to a greased 9×5×3-inch loaf pan.

Place the pan in the oven and bake for 1 hour or until done. Remove the pan from the oven and cool for 10 minutes. Remove the bread from the pan and cool on a rack.

Yield: 1 loaf

Heat Scale: Medium

Dried Cherry Ancho Orange Muffins

Here's one of the most unusual bread recipes in this chapter, one that combines the fruity flavors of cherries and oranges, not to mention the raisiny overtones of the ancho chiles. Serve these for breakfast topped with honey.

1 cup sugar	2 teaspoons ancho chile powder
½ cup margarine	1 cup low-fat buttermilk
2 eggs	1 cup dried tart cherries, chopped
Zest of one orange	1 orange, juiced
2 cups all-purpose flour	1 tablespoon sugar
½ teaspoon salt	
1 teaspoon baking soda	

Preheat oven to 400 degrees. In a medium mixing bowl, cream the sugar and margarine with an electric mixer until smooth. Add the eggs and zest, then continue to beat until the mixture becomes fluffy.

In a separate bowl, combine the flour, salt, baking soda, and ancho powder. Add the flour mixture to the creamed mixture alternately with the buttermilk. Add the cherries to the batter and mix well. Pour the batter into a greased muffin tin, filling each cup about three-quarters full. Bake the muffins in the oven for 20 minutes.

When the muffins are done, remove the pan to a wire rack. Brush the muffins with the orange juice and sprinkle sugar on them while they are still warm. Let the muffins sit in the pan for at least 5 minutes before serving.

Yield: 6 large muffins

Heat Scale: Medium

Pasilla Carrot Zucchini Bread

Also known as the *chilaca* pepper in its fresh form, this pasilla pepper offers a rich, raisiny hot flavor that is sure to liven up this moist bread.

3	eggs	3	cups all-purpose flour
1	cup vegetable oil	1	teaspoon salt
2½	cups sugar	½	teaspoon baking powder
1	cup grated zucchini	1	tablepoon cinnamon
1	cup grated carrots	½	cup chopped nuts
2½	teaspoons vanilla extract		
2	pasilla chiles, seeds and stems removed, minced		

Preheat the oven to 350 degrees. In a large bowl, beat the eggs. Add the oil, sugar, zucchini, carrots, vanilla, and pasillas. Combine the flour, salt, baking powder, and cinnamon in a separate bowl, then slowly add to the zucchini mixture, mixing well. Stir in the nuts.

  Pour the batter into 2 greased loaf pans and bake for 1 hour. Make sure you do not overbake, or the bread will be dry.

Yield: 2 loaves

Heat Scale: Medium

Chile in the West

"When the diminishing light of winter begins to get to me, I put some chopped chile in my scrambled eggs, breathing its inimitable *calor* through a runny nose. I don't question the assumption that chiles cure everything from hangovers to asthma. I don't question chiles at all. They grow where lettuce fears to tread, wilting and unloved in crummy soil, but ultimately successful. I can't conceive of living in the West and not growing chile."

          Robin Chotzinoff

Cultured Blackberry Cornbread

We call this cornbread "cultured" because one of the main ingredients is nonfat yogurt! We've added some red chile powder and orange zest to ensure the best-tasting cornbread around.

1 cup fine-grind blue cornmeal	Zest of one large orange
1 cup unbleached all-purpose flour	2 eggs
2 tablespoons sugar	¼ cup low-fat buttermilk
½ teaspoon salt	1¼ cups plain nonfat yogurt
2 teaspoons New Mexican red chile powder	1½ cups rinsed blackberries
½ teaspoon baking soda	¼ cup safflower oil

Preheat the oven to 425 degrees. In a large mixing bowl, combine the cornmeal, flour, sugar, salt, red chile powder, baking soda, and orange zest. Combine the mixture well, then set aside.

In a smaller bowl, combine the eggs, buttermilk, and yogurt with a whisk. Add the wet mixture to the dry ingredients, and gently fold in the blackberries. Pour the oil over the top of the batter. Stir gently until all the ingredients are mixed. Be careful not to overmix.

Pour the batter into a greased 8-inch springform pan. Bake for 20 or 25 minutes, until browned and firm to the touch. Let stand at least 15 minutes before serving.

Yield: 1 (8-inch) cornbread

Heat Scale: Medium

Heavenly Green Chile Pineapple Banana Bread

This bread is heavenly because it's light as air in both texture and calories. It tastes good *and* is good for you—imagine that!

1⅔	cups whole wheat flour	1	cup mashed banana
1	teaspoon baking soda	½	cup pineapple chunks
½	teaspoon salt	3	green chiles, stemmed, seeded, and chopped
½	cup margarine, softened		
1	cup sugar	¼	cup low-fat milk
2	eggs	1	tablespoon lemon juice
1	teaspoon vanilla extract	½	cup chopped walnuts

Preheat the oven to 350 degrees. Grease a loaf pan and set aside. In a small mixing bowl, combine the flour, baking soda, and salt. In a large bowl, beat the margarine, sugar, eggs, and vanilla with an electric mixer until it is fluffy. Slowly add the flour mixture, using the mixer, then add the banana, pineapple chunks, chiles, and milk. Add the lemon juice and walnuts and mix for a final 30 seconds. Pour the batter in the loaf pan. Bake for 1 hour, making sure not to overcook.

Yield: 1 loaf

Heat Scale: Medium

Red Chile Croutons

These not-so-traditional croutons will spice up any salad. Make sure you keep them in an airtight bag, and they will stay fresh for up to two weeks. These also work well as a breading for eggplant parmigiana.

4 cups cubed sourdough bread	2 teaspoons New Mexican
4 tablespoons margarine, melted	red chile powder

Spread the sourdough cubes on a cookie sheet. Combine the melted butter and red chile powder, then pour the mixture over the bread cubes. Bake in an oven at 400 degrees for 5 minutes, then stir. Bake for another 5 to 10 minutes, or until crisp.

Yield: 4 cups

Heat Scale: Hot

On Bread

"Without bread all is misery."

William Cobbett

"The smell of good bread baking, like the sound of lightly flowing water, is indescribable in its evocation of innocence and delight."

M. F. K. Fisher

"Bread is the king of the table and all else is merely the court that surround the king. The countries are the soup, the meat, the vegetables, the salad . . . but bread is king."

Louis Bromfield

"The smell of buttered toast simply talked to Toad, and with no uncertain voice; talked of warm kitchens, of breakfasts on bright frosty mornings, of cosy parlour firesides on winter evenings."

Kenneth Grahame

Red Chile Twists

Don't tell anyone how easy these twists are to make! They are delicate and delicious, and people assume they are difficult to make. Make several batches at a time, as they are very fast to put together and they freeze beautifully.

1	package frozen puff pastry dough or homemade puff pastry, thawed	¼	cup unsalted butter, melted
		1	teaspoon red chile powder

Preheat the oven to 400 degrees.

    Roll out the pastry dough on a lightly floured surface. With a pastry wheel or sharp knife, cut the dough in strips. Lightly brush the dough with melted butter, then lightly sprinkle the red chile powder on top. Twist each strip in a spiral and place on a baking sheet. Place the baking sheet in the refrigerator for 15 minutes to cool the dough. Remove from the refrigerator and bake for 15 to 20 minutes or until lightly browned.

Yield: 4 to 6 servings

Heat Scale: Medium

No Bake Habanero Ricotta Cheese Hearts

These biscuits of sorts look so innocent. However, they definitely have a heat level worth bragging about with the addition of the world's hottest pepper, the habanero.

1 cup low-fat ricotta cheese	¼ habanero chile, seeds and stem removed, minced
3 tablespoons plain nonfat yogurt	½ teaspoon almond extract
1 tablespoon honey	6 sprigs mint

Combine the ricotta, yogurt, honey, habanero, and almond extract in a food processor until smooth and fluffy. Be careful not to overprocess.

Divide the cheese mixture into 6 individual heart-shaped porcelain molds lined with two layers of rinsed cheesecloth. Fold the cheesecloth over the cheese mixture and press gently. Place the molds on a tray to catch the drippings, and cover with plastic wrap. Refrigerate the molds overnight.

To serve, fold back the cheesecloth and gently turn each heart out onto a small plate. Garnish with a sprig of mint and serve immediately.

Yield: 6 cheese biscuits

Heat Scale: Hot

Note: This recipe requires advanced preparation.

Habanero Cheese Straws

We thank Denice Skrepcinski for this recipe. Cheese straws are delicate cheese- and chile-flavored crackers. In the South, everyone looks for the tin containing cheese straws when they attend a party or family gathering. It is a little difficult to get the dough to the perfect consistency and to bake them without browning them; it takes a little practice to master, but they are well worth the effort. Store the cheese straws in a tightly covered container. These also freeze very well. If the habanero powder is too hot for your taste, substitute cayenne powder.

½   cup unsalted butter, softened
4   ounces sharp cheddar cheese, finely grated
4   ounces Parmesan cheese, finely grated
1   teaspoon salt
¼   teaspoon habanero powder
1¾   to 2¼ cups flour

Preheat the oven to 375 degrees. Lightly grease baking sheets and set aside. In a large bowl, thoroughly mix the butter, cheddar cheese, and Parmesan cheese. Make sure the mixture is very smooth. Add the salt and habanero powder. Add the flour ½ cup at a time until the dough comes together.

      Divide the dough in half. Roll out one half of the dough until it is ¼-inch thick. With a pastry wheel or sharp knife, cut the dough into strips that are 3 inches long and 1 inch wide. Place on the baking sheets. Bake for 7 to 10 minutes. Watch them carefully and be sure they do not get too brown. Remove straws from oven and let cool on a wire rack.

Yield: About 50 straws

Heat Scale: Hot

Cheddar-Charged Chile Biscuits

These rich and delicious biscuits only take a minute to make and are a tasteful accompaniment to any of the soups in Chapter 4 or the salads in Chapter 3.

2   jalapeño chiles, seeds and stems removed, chopped, or ¼ cup chopped New Mexican green chile

2   cups unbleached flour

4   teaspoons baking powder

3   tablespoons butter

½   cup low-fat milk

¼   cup whole milk

¼   cup light cream

1   cup shredded sharp cheddar cheese

2   tablespoons chopped fresh chives

Preheat the oven to 425 degrees. Over medium heat, heat a small skillet and add the chile; dry sauté the chile slowly to release the excess moisture, stirring to avoid burning. Remove from the heat and set aside to cool.

In a medium bowl, sift the flour and baking powder together and cut in the butter using your fingers or a pastry cutter. Mix in the cooled chiles. Add the milk and cream and lightly stir into the flour mixture, using as few strokes as possible. Add the cheese and the chives, lightly stirring until the mixture is blended. Do not overmix, or the biscuits will be tough.

Turn the dough onto a lightly floured board and pat or lightly roll the dough to a ½-inch thickness. Using a 2-inch or 3-inch cutter, cut the dough into rounds and place on an oiled cookie sheet.

Bake for 15 to 20 minutes, until the biscuits are golden-brown. Serve immediately.

Yield: 8 to 10 biscuits

Heat Scale: Mild

Chile Cheese Puffs

These traditional cheese puffs, French *gougères*, are given a hot new twist with the addition of hot sauce or ground red chile. This recipe is a rich one (butter and eggs)—make it for a splurge luncheon or dinner! They can be served with additional red chile butter, or even filled with a salad. Try them filled with Spicy, Urbane Mac and Cheese from Chapter 6.

1 cup milk	4 eggs
¼ cup butter	1 cup shredded low-fat Swiss cheese or low-fat Jarlsberg cheese
½ teaspoon salt	
⅛ teaspoon freshly ground white pepper	
1 cup unsifted unbleached flour	
1 teaspoon habanero hot sauce or 2 teaspoons pure red ground chile	

Preheat the oven to 375 degrees. Heat the milk, butter, salt, and pepper in a 2-quart saucepan to a full boil, then add the flour all at once. Reduce the heat to medium and stir for about 2 minutes, or until the mixture leaves the pan and forms a ball.

Remove the pan from the heat, add the hot sauce, and, by hand, beat in the eggs one at a time until the mixture is smooth and well blended. Beat in ½ cup of the cheese.

Using an ice cream scoop or a large spoon, make 7 equal balls of dough in a circle on a greased cookie sheet, using about three-quarters of the dough. Each ball of dough should just touch the next one.

With the remaining dough, place a small mound of dough on top of each larger mound. Sprinkle the remaining 1/2 cup of the cheese over the dough mounds.

Bake for 50 to 55 minutes, or until the puffs are lightly browned and crisp. Serve hot, or cool the puffs on a rack and fill.

Yield: 7 puffs

Heat Scale: Mild

Green Chile and Goat Cheese Muffins

These muffins are perfect for a picnic when accompanied by fresh fruit or our Peppered Pineapple Fruit Salad with Cayenne Turnips from Chapter 3.

2¼ cups all-purpose flour
2 tablespoons yellow cornmeal
2 teaspoons baking powder
Dash salt
1 cup skim milk
¼ cup olive oil
2 eggs
½ cup coarsely chopped pitted black olives

3 New Mexican green chiles, roasted, peeled, seeds and stems removed, chopped
¼ cup drained oil-packed sun dried tomatoes, chopped
6 ounces round herbed goat cheese, cut into 9 wedges and rolled into balls
9 pecan halves

Preheat the oven to 375 degrees. Grease 9 standard-size muffin cups. In a large mixing bowl, combine the flour, cornmeal, baking powder, and salt, then set aside. In another mixing bowl, whisk together the milk, olive oil, and eggs. Pour the egg mixture into the flour mixture and stir with a wooden spoon until just moistened. Gently fold in the olives, chiles, and sun-dried tomatoes. The batter should not look smooth.

Fill each muffin cup half-full with the batter. Press a ball of the cheese on top of the batter in each cup. Spoon the rest of the olive batter equally into each muffin cup. Place a pecan half on top of each muffin.

Bake the muffins in the center of the oven for about 24 minutes, or until the muffins are brown but not overbaked. Remove the muffins from the oven and let them rest in the pan for 5 minutes. After they have cooled initially, turn them out onto a wire rack.

Yield: 9 muffins

Heat Scale: Medium

Jazzy Carrot Ancho Muffins

These muffins will definitely perk up your taste buds, especially if you serve them for breakfast or a brunch. They have plenty of flavor and lots of crunch. The muffins freeze well and can be made ahead of time, later to be thawed and lighted warmed in the oven.

½ cup unbleached or all-purpose flour	⅓ cup canola or safflower oil
2 cups whole wheat pastry flour	½ cup chile honey
2 teaspoons baking powder	1¼ cups grated carrots, drained of excess moisture
¼ teaspoon salt	⅓ cup chopped walnuts or pecans
3 tablespoons ancho chile powder	2 tablespoons lightly toasted sesame seeds
2 eggs beaten or an egg substitute, at room temperature	½ cup raisins or currants
1 cup low-fat milk, at room temperature	

Preheat the oven to 400 degrees. Combine the flours, baking powder, salt, and chile powder in a medium bowl.

In a small bowl, blend together the eggs, milk, oil, and honey. Pour this mixture into the flour mixture and stir briefly. Carefully fold in the carrots, walnuts, sesame seeds, and raisins, taking care not to overmix.

Place 12 paper muffin cups (bake cups) into a muffin tin, and spoon ½ cup of the mix into each of the paper cups.

Bake for 15 to 20 minutes, or until the muffins are lightly browned on top. Cool on a wire rack.

Yield: 12 muffins

Heat Scale: Mild

Sweet Potato–Cayenne Dinner Rolls

Thanks to Denice Skrepcinski for creating this recipe. She describes it as "hearty, pretty, and with a hint of pepper; these rolls are great to serve with any dinner." She also says that they would be wonderful for a holiday dinner. They also make great sandwiches with the addition of grilled vegetables and mushrooms and sliced provolone cheese.

4¾ cups bread flour	2 tablespoons shortening
1 tablespoon sugar	¾ cups cooked and mashed sweet potatoes
1 tablepoon salt	
1 teaspoon cayenne powder	1 egg lightly beaten with 1 teaspoon water
2 packages active dry yeast	
2 cups water	

Grease two 8-inch round cake pans and set aside. In a large mixing bowl, combine 3½ cups of the flour, sugar, salt, cayenne, and yeast and mix well. In a saucepan, heat the 2 cups water and shortening until the temperature is 120 to 130 degrees. Add the warm liquid to the flour mixture. Stir or use a mixer to combine, then add the mashed sweet potatoes. Add the remaining flour one half cup at a time until dough is smooth and elastic. (Not all the flour may need to be added.)

Divide the dough into 16 pieces. Shape each piece of dough into a ball. Place 8 of the balls into a greased cake pan. Repeat with remaining dough and second cake pan. Cover loosely with kitchen towel and let dough rise until it doubles in size. Heat oven to 375 degrees. Brush rolls with egg wash and bake for 20 to 30 minutes or until golden brown.

Yield: 16 rolls

Heat Scale: Mild

Positively Pungent Pasilla Bread

This unusual bread is worth the time. The cornmeal adds an interesting texture, and the pasilla chiles give the bread a raisiny overtone. If you have a bread machine or a food processor with a dough hook, use it for this recipe. Set your bread machine on the Manual setting and let it do the kneading for you.

5½	to 6½ cups unsifted unbleached flour	4	tablespoons butter or margarine, cut into small pieces
2½	teaspoons salt		
1	cup yellow cornmeal	2	cups very hot water
2	packages yeast	½	cup molasses
		¼	cup pasilla chile powder

Mix 2½ cups of the flour, salt, cornmeal, and yeast in a large bowl and add the butter. Gradually add the water and molasses and beat for 2 minutes with an electric mixer at medium speed. Add ½ cup of the remaining flour and beat at high speed for 2 minutes. Stir in enough additional flour to make a soft dough.

Turn the dough out onto a floured board and knead it for 8 to 10 minutes, until it is smooth and elastic. Or, place the dough in your bread machine or food processor (with a dough hook) and set the timer for 8 minutes and let your machine do the work.

Place the kneaded dough into a greased bowl, turn it to grease the top, cover, and let it rise in a warm place for 1 hour or until it doubles in size.

Punch the dough down, turn onto a floured board, divide the dough in half, shape into loaves, and place each loaf into a greased pan, 8×4×2 ½ or 9×5×3. Cover the pans and let the dough rise in a warm place until it doubles in size, about 45 minutes.

Preheat the oven to 375 degrees. Bake for 30 to 35 minutes. Remove the bread from the pans and cool on a rack.

Yield: 2 loaves

Heat Scale: Mild

The Chiles' Fiery Flavors

Chef Mark Miller of the Coyote Cafe in Santa Fe has assembled a list of forty-one "Chile Flavor Descriptors," which are divided into the categories of "fruity" and "other flavors." The fruity flavors included citrusy (particularly orange and lemon), which would apply to most varieties of habaneros and some of the yellow South American *ajís*, and raisin, which is the ever-present aroma of the anchos and pasillas. Other fruity descriptors were black cherry, fig, mango, and melon. In the other flavors category, Miller lists chocolate, tobacco, tannic, soapy, green tea, and—how ironic—black pepper.

Unfortunately, the science of chile flavors is still in its infancy, and most of the hundreds of chile varieties have not yet been matched to their flavor descriptors. However, chile chefs on the edge will certainly do more research into this important facet of chile flavor.

Quick Chipotle Casserole Bread

When you want to make some interesting bread fast, try this recipe. The chipotle chile gives the bread an interesting light brown hue and a most unique taste. We have had the most success baking the bread in a round, ovenproof glass casserole dish.

1	cup milk	2	packages yeast
3	tablespoons sugar	1	chipotle chile in adobo sauce, minced
1	tablespoon salt		
1½	tablespoons shortening	4½	cups flour
1	cup warm water		

Scald the milk and stir in the sugar, salt, and shortening. Cool until the mixture is lukewarm.

In a large bowl, measure the warm water, sprinkle the yeast over the water, and stir until the yeast dissolves. Stir in the milk mixture and the chipotle chile.

Add the flour a little at a time and stir until the mixture is well blended. Cover and let the mixture rise for 40 minutes or until the batter doubles in size.

Preheat the oven to 375 degrees. Stir the batter down and beat the batter for 1 minute. Grease a 1½-quart casserole. Pour the bread batter into the casserole.

Bake for about 1 hour, or until the bread is golden-brown. Let the bread cool on a rack several minutes before slicing, and use a serrated knife to slice it.

Yield: 1 loaf

Heat Scale: Mild

Seriously Serrano Dill Bread

We have all had some version of this bread at some time in our lives. However, we have livened up the traditional family recipe by adding some serrano chiles to add a little punch to the onion and the dill. It is good served warm, but you need to allow it to cool slightly, otherwise slicing it will be a nightmare.

1	cup cottage cheese, drained and at room temperature	1	teaspoon salt
2	tablespoons sugar	¼	teaspoon baking soda
½	cup or more chopped onion	2	eggs, at room temperature
1	tablespoon dill weed	1	package dry yeast
2	tablespoons chopped serrano chiles	2½	cups flour
		½	teaspoon melted butter
		¼	teaspoon Kosher salt

Heat the cottage cheese in a saucepan until it is warm to the touch. Pour the cottage cheese into a mixer bowl and add the sugar, onion, dill, serrano chiles, salt, baking soda, eggs, and yeast.

Add the flour, ½ cup at a time, to make a stiff batter, beating well after each addition with a mixer or wooden spoon. Cover the dough with plastic wrap and let rise for 1 hour. Remove the plastic wrap and stir down the batter for 30 seconds.

Pour the batter into a greased 1-quart casserole. Cover with wax paper and leave until batter doubles in volume, about 45 minutes. Keep the wax paper from touching the expanding batter.

Preheat the oven to 350 degrees about 20 minutes before baking. Bake the bread until it is deep brown and crusty, about 35 to 45 minutes. Cover with foil for the last 15 minutes.

Remove the bread from the oven and brush with the butter and sprinkle on the salt. Cool the bread for about 10 minutes before removing it from the casserole.

Yield: 1 loaf

Heat Scale: Medium

Science Solves Some Chile Puzzles

A person suffering from ulcers should never eat chile—right or wrong? Why can some people eat hot chiles and others cannot?

Finally, we're getting the answers to some of these questions. Regarding the ulcer inquiry, investigators at the National University Hospital in Singapore examined the inner lining of the stomach with sophisticated technology to investigate the causes of peptic ulcers. "A lot of people feel that a pepper is bad for their ulcers and their stomach," said Dr. Jin Y. Kang. "We've shown that it does not harm the stomach and may even help."

The scientists gave patients temporary gut damage with irritants such as aspirin or alcohol, then applied capsaicin to the damaged areas. Rather than aggravating the damage, capsaicin somehow eased the irritation.

The scientists speculated that capsaicin stimulates nerve fibers that release a hormone that increases blood flow to the area and helps to protect the stomach from irritants. But they insist that diluted capsaicin—not the peppers themselves— would be the most efficacious.

The reason some people cannot eat hot chiles is simple, really. They are called supertasters and have nearly twice the number of taste buds per centimeter of tongue area. Approximately one-fourth of the population are supertasters, while half has normal taste, and another fourth are called nontasters because of their lack of taste buds. The supertasters are acutely sensitive to sweet, spicy, and bitter tastes and hence have less tolerance to chiles. Nontasters can enter chile-eating contests, and often do.

Firewater and Cooldown Desserts

When we say firewater, we mean it—in two ways! First is the traditional meaning of alcoholic beverages and second is the chiles that we fire them up with. Our first three drinks will amaze you with their dual power. Chile-Flavored Vodka (p. 236) is our version of the chile-flavored vodkas such as Absolut Pepper and Stolichnaya's Pertsovka, except, of course, that we use three different chiles to heat it up. We've tried this recipe with tequila, and it works great. Mitch Moody's "Red Ass" Bloody Mary Mix (p. 237) only has two kinds of chiles, but he claims that it makes the greatest Bloody Mary on the face of the earth. Margarita lovers will flip for our Jalapeño Margarita (p. 238) from the Scottsdale Princess resort in Arizona. Rounding out our alcoholic drinks is a non-chile after-dinner favorite, Coffee-Banana Alexander (p. 241), which combines rum, espresso, bananas, and milk.

We warn readers that our obsession with chiles has required us to add them to a few drinks and desserts—but only a few. The rest of these recipes were created to refresh the palate after a fiery meal. Moving on to non-alcoholic drinks, two of our favorites are Passionate Fruit Punch (p. 239) with passion fruit, lime, grape, and pineapple to create a refreshing drink for a hot summer afternoon. Equally refreshing—and unusual—is Refresco de Arroz, Ecuadorian Rice Drink (p. 240), which was collected for us by David Parrish.

On to desserts and one ingredient that is always controversial: sugar. For years, we've heard that sugar is evil, but as usual, the warnings are highly exaggerated. A recent study by Duke University concluded what we've always suspected: that sugar has gotten a bum rap over the years. The researchers found no links between sugar and diabetes, obesity, hyperactivity, depression, or anxiety. The real problem is the company sugar keeps in foods, namely fat. As one newspaper editorial put it, "It's not the brown sugar in oatmeal cookies that puts on the pounds; it's the shortening." Sugar better be okay for you—the average American consumes forty-three pounds of it a year!

We love fruits, as is evident by Tropical Compote in Sweet Tortilla Cups (p. 242), with oranges, mangos, and strawberries. And speaking of berries, Summer Berry Dessert (p. 244) features berries of blue, black, rasp, and straw. And our love of fruits extends to sorbets with Mango-Habanero Sorbet (p. 245), where the fruitiness of the habanero complements the mango. Another great sorbet is made, surprisingly, not with a fruit but with a squash. Pumpkin Sorbet (p. 246) is flavored with almond liqueur.

Three more unusual dessert recipes feature flavors from around the world. Cardamom Cake (p. 247) is Scandinavian in origin, while Bisteeya

(p. 248) is a Moroccan pastry that can also be served as a side dish. Guava Duff (p. 250) is the national dessert of the Bahamas and is spiced with nutmeg, cinnamon, and cloves.

Chocolate lovers can rejoice with the following three recipes that feature the flavor of cacao. Tropical Fruit Crepes with Chocolate (p. 251) mixes chocolate with minced fruits such as papaya, mango, kiwi fruit, red bananas, blood oranges, and melons, so it's the cook's choice. We've taken the liberty to transform Mexican wedding cake into Mexican Chocolate and Piñon Wedding Cookies (p. 252), but we still use the cinnamon-flavored Ibarra chocolate. The Hawaiian Vintage Chocolate Soufflé (p. 253) features the only chocolate produced in the United States, Hawaiian Vintage. If it is not available, use the next most expensive chocolate you can find for this dessert.

Imagine eating a daiquiri as a pastry, and you'll essentially have our Daiquiri Tarts (p. 254). Another of our favorites is Apple Crisp with Raisins and Vanilla Yogurt Topping (p. 255), flavored with honey, nutmeg, cinnamon, and allspice.

We have strived for low-fat flavor in this book, but we confess to one excess, Flan à la Antigua (p. 256). Save it for your one excess every year—or is that every week? However, we completely redeem ourselves with Relatively Low-Fat Hot Chocolate Pudding (p. 257), in which we do everything we can to lower the fat without depleting the flavor.

Chile-Flavored Vodka

When we write "flavored," we mean it, as we have chosen the chiles that we think impart the most distinct flavors. The raisiny flavor of the pasilla melds with the apricot overtones of the habanero and the earthiness of the New Mexican chile to create a finely tuned fiery sipping vodka. Of course, use an excellent vodka like Stolichnaya or Absolut.

1   liter vodka

1   pasilla chile, seeds and stems removed, cut into thin strips

½   dried red New Mexican chile pod, seeds and stems removed, cut in fourths

¼   habanero chile, seeds and stems removed, left whole

Open the bottle of vodka and drink some of it to make room in the bottle. Add the chiles and recap. Let sit for at least 3 days to generate some heat; the vodka will get progressively hotter over the weeks. As you drink the vodka, replace it with more fresh vodka, and the process will go on for some time.

Yield: About 1 quart

Heat Scale: Varies

"Red Ass" Bloody Mary Mix

So named because of his chili team, Mitch "Red Ass Chili" Moody of Long Beach, California explained the origin of this particular drink mix that appeared in *Chile Pepper* magazine: "A lot of chili cook-offs start this way or at least ours do! This mix will spice up your morning and possibly help with that hangover from the night before. I got the idea from a friend who told me about *sangrita*, a chaser that is served with tequila shots. Delete the habanero unless you like it extremely hot! I've heard that the mix is also good without alcohol, but I've never tried it that way."

1	jalapeño chile, stem and seeds removed	1	teaspoon freshly ground black pepper
1	habanero chile, stem and seeds removed	¼	teaspoon dried oregano
			Juice of ½ lemon
6	tablespoons Worcestershire sauce	1	cup orange juice
¼	cup A-1 sauce	1	quart tomato juice
2	tablespoons chopped fresh cilantro		Salt
			Mild chile powder
1	tablespoon horseradish		Lemon or lime slices
1	tablespoon garlic salt		Vodka or tequila

Put the chiles, Worcestershire sauce, A-1 sauce, cilantro, horseradish, garlic salt, pepper, and oregano in a blender and process until smooth. Stir in the juices and chill.

To serve, place the salt and chile powder on a plate. Wet the rim of the serving glasses with a lime slice and rub the glass upside down on the salt mixture. Pour 1½ ounces of liquor in each glass along with ice, fill with the Bloody Mary mix, stir well, garnish with a lime slice, and serve.

Yield: 1 quart

Heat Scale: Hot

Jalapeño Margarita

According to *Chile Pepper* author Donald Downes, Scottsdale Princess executive chef Reed Groban "got all fired-up about chiles after moving from the East about nine years ago to head the resort's kitchens." Reed is proud that his beverage department developed a jalapeño margarita, certainly a unique capsicum cocktail.

1¼ ounces Hornitos tequila	1½ ounces lime juice
¾ ounce Triple Sec	Dash of Tabasco Jalapeño Sauce
2 ounces Hot and Sour Mix (see Note below)	Lime slice and whole jalapeño

Place all ingredients, except lime slice and whole jalapeño, in a blender; blend to mix. Pour over ice and garnish with the lime slice and whole jalapeño. If a frozen margarita is preferred, add 1 cup ice to blender with other ingredients.

Yield: 1 serving

Heat Scale: Medium

Notes: This recipe requires advance preparation. To make Hot and Sour Mix: add to one quart of sour mix 4 large jalapeños, stems and seeds removed, diced. Let steep for at least 24 hours.

Passionate Fruit Punch

With more tropical fruits becoming available in North American markets, it's a great opportunity to utilize them in recipes of all kinds. If fresh passion fruits are not available, use the concentrate that's available from Bello brand of the island of Dominica in the West Indies. Of course, it would be permissible to add a bit of rum to this punch.

½ cup passion fruit juice, made from the pulp of fresh passion fruits, or substitute ¼ cup concentrate

¼ cup freshly squeezed lime juice

3 cups white grape juice

2 cups pineapple juice

2 (12-ounce) cans ginger ale

Lime slices

Combine all ingredients, except lime slices. Serve in tall glasses filled with crushed ice and garnish with lime slices.

Yield: 4 to 6 servings

Heat Scale: Mild

Great Moments in the History of Beverages

- 3000 B.C.: Wine supplants beer as the drink of choice in Mesopotamia.
- 1554: The first coffeehouse opens for business in Constantinople, Turkey.
- 1640: First rum distilled from sugar cane, Barbados, West Indies (some say 1703).
- 1814: Commercial distillation of Scotch whiskey begins in Scotland.
- 1886: Coca Cola first sold in Atlanta, Georgia.
- 1944: The Mai Tai invented at Trader Vic's in Oakland, California.
- 1952: Irish Coffee invented at the Buena Vista Cafe in San Francisco.

Refresco de Arroz (Ecuadorian Rice Drink)

This recipe is from David Parrish, who wrote on Ecuador for *Chile Pepper* magazine. He commented: "This very tasty and nutritious drink was served to me on a friend's farm outside of Quito. It's an Indian drink and actually can be made with almost any grain, even oats."

2	cups uncooked rice		2	cups sugar
2	quarts cold water		1	(2-inch) stick cinnamon
2	cups orange juice or any fruit juice			

Place the rice in a blender or spice mill and grind to a powder. Combine with the water and cook over a medium heat, stirring occasionally, for an hour, adding more water (up to 6 cups) if needed.

When the rice is soft, strain through a fine sieve, allowing the liquid to drain into a large container and cool. Save 1 cup of the rice mush and discard the rest.

Combine juice, sugar, and cinnamon in a saucepan. Simmer, stirring occasionally, until the mixture becomes a syrup, about 15 to 20 minutes. Discard the cinnamon stick.

Place the reserved rice mush in a blender and process until it is smooth and creamy. Add this and the syrup to the rice liquid. Stir thoroughly and let cool overnight in the refrigerator.

Dilute, if needed, with water to desired consistency—usually it is the consistency of a citrus juice, or perhaps somewhat thicker. Serve cold.

Yield: 2 to 3 quarts

Heat Scale: Mild

Note: This recipe requires advance preparation.

Coffee-Banana Alexander

Here's an unusual, tropical twist on the Brandy Alexander that combines coffee, bananas, and rum. Serve it as an after-dinner drink or a thin dessert.

1	cup cold espresso	½	cup crushed ice
2	cups milk	2	ripe bananas
1	cup dark rum		Ground allspice

Combine the espresso, milk, rum, ice, and bananas in a blender and process until smooth. Pour into tall glasses and sprinkle with allspice.

Yield: 4 servings

Heat Scale: Mild

Great Moments in the History of Desserts

- 38,000 B.C.: Prehistoric humankind in Europe collects honey from wild beehives.
- 2,000 B.C.: Watermelons first cultivated in Africa.
- c. 1200: Invention of ice cream in China.
- 1523: The European conqueror Cortez is introduced to chocolate by the Aztec emperor Montezuma.
- 1830: A French botanist named Neumann perfects the artificial pollination of vanilla, ensuring its commercial cultivation.
- 1906: Invention of the Hot Fudge Sundae, C. C. Brown's restaurant, Hollywood, California.
- 1949: Both Pillsbury and General Mills introduce the first prepared cake mixes in chocolate, gold, and white.

Tropical Compote in Sweet Tortilla Cups

This recipe is from Nancy Gerlach, who wrote in *Chile Pepper*: "Adding spices, seasonings, and chile to flour tortilla recipes is becoming very popular in New Mexico; here, I've added cinnamon and sugar. These tortillas can then be baked or fried to make an edible plate for this dessert."

Tortillas:

2   tablespoons sugar

1   tablespoon ground cinnamon

4   flour tortillas

To bake the cups: Preheat the oven to 375 degrees. Warm the tortillas to soften them. Lightly brush one side of a tortilla with butter or margarine. Combine the sugar and cinnamon and sprinkle onto the flour tortillas. Press tortillas, butter side down, into a large muffin tin or in ovenproof bowls or custard cups. Place the bowls on a pan and bake for 10 minutes or until the tortillas are golden.

To fry the cups: In a deep-fat fryer, heat the vegetable oil to 375 degrees. Place the tortilla in the oil and press it down to the bottom with a 6-ounce ladle and hold for 30 seconds until the tortilla is golden. Remove and drain.

Compote:

2   large oranges, cut in segments without any white membrane

1   large mango, peeled and sliced, or use canned mango

2   cups strawberries

½   cup sugar

¼   cup orange-flavored liqueur

½   cup whipping cream

2   tablespoons powdered sugar plus additional for garnish

Sliced almonds

In a bowl, layer the fruits with the sugar and liqueur and refrigerate for 2 hours to blend the flavors.

Whip the cream and powdered sugar until soft peaks form.

To assemble, place the tortilla cup on a plate, ladle in the fruit, put a dollop of cream on the top, and garnish with almonds and powdered sugar.

Variation: The tortillas can be fried flat for a fruit tostada. Serve as above.

Yield: 4 servings

Heat Scale: Mild

Note: This recipe requires advance preparation.

On Dessert

"Dessert comes from the French word *desservir,* which means to remove all the dishes from the table to make room for the final course, the fruit or cake served to sweeten the palate."

Martin Elkhort

"The dessert is said to be to the dinner what the madrigal is to literature—it is the light poetry of the kitchen."

George Ellwanger

"I doubt whether the world holds for anyone a more soul-stirring surprise that the first adventure with ice cream."

Heywood Broun

"The most dangerous dessert is wedding cake."

American proverb

Summer Berry Dessert

Here is a combination dessert that features those wonderful berries of the summertime. Any combination of berries will work here—we just particularly like this mixture. To toast the coconut, simply heat it in a dry skillet, stirring constantly. This is enough to serve a medium dinner party.

1	pint blueberries	¾	cup raspberry liqueur or concentrate
1	pint blackberries, coarsely chopped		Toasted grated coconut
1	pint raspberries, coarsely chopped		Mango-Habanero Sorbet (see recipe, p. 245)
1	pint strawberries, coarsely chopped		Mexican Chocolate and Piñon Wedding Cookies (see recipe, p. 252)
	Juice of 1 lemon		

In a bowl, combine the berries, lemon juice, and liqueur. Cover and refrigerate the mixture for 1 hour to blend the flavors.

To serve, scoop the berry mixture onto a dessert plate and sprinkle toasted coconut over the top. Add a scoop of the sorbet and 2 cookies.

Yield: 12 servings

Heat Scale: Varies with the amount of sorbet

Note: This recipe requires advance preparation.

Mango-Habanero Sorbet

We've added just a hint of habanero to give this sorbet a sweet heat punch. Of course, non-chileheads can eliminate it for a purist's dessert. To make a refreshing drink with this sorbet, combine 2 tablespoons of it with 1 teaspoon Triple Sec over ice and top with sparkling water. Stir well.

¾ cup water

6 tablespoons sugar

3 cups freshly squeezed orange juice

3 tablespoons orange liqueur, such as Triple Sec

¼ habanero chile, seeds and stems removed, minced

In a saucepan, bring the water and sugar to a boil, stirring well to dissolve the sugar. Pour into a 9-inch cake pan and let cool. Stir in the orange juice, liqueur, and the habanero and cover. Place in the freezer and freeze solid, about 2 hours.

Break into chunks and beat with an electric mixer or blender until slushy. Use immediately or process in an ice cream freezer.

Yield: 6 servings

Heat Scale: Medium

Note: This recipe requires advance preparation.

Pumpkin Sorbet

There are plenty of fruit sorbets, but you can make them out of vegetables as well. Since pumpkin makes a splendid pie, it follows that it makes a great sorbet as well.

1 (16-ounce) can solid-pack pumpkin	½ cup sugar
	Dash salt
¾ cup freshly squeezed orange juice	1 cup almond-flavored liqueur, such as Amaretto
1 teaspoon lemon juice	Mint leaves

In a bowl, combine the pumpkin, orange juice, lemon juice, sugar, and salt. Pour the mixture into ice cube trays and freeze solid. Dip the trays in warm water to release the cubes.

Place half the cubes and half the liqueur in a blender or food processor and puree until smooth. Repeat, using the remaining cubes and liqueur.

Serve in bowls garnished with the mint leaves.

Yield: 8 to 10 servings

Heat Scale: Mild

Note: This recipe requires advance preparation.

Cardamom Cake

Melody Favish, who wrote about spicy Scandinavia in *Chile Pepper* magazine, collected this recipe. "This spiced pound cake can be served on its own with a cup of tea or as a dessert with ice cream and fruit," she noted.

¾	cup unsalted butter, at room temperature	1⅔	cups cake flour
1	cup sugar	1	teaspoon baking powder
3	eggs	4	teaspoons ground cardamom
⅓	cup whipping cream	1	teaspoon grated lemon rind

Preheat the oven to 350 degrees. Lightly oil and flour a 8×4-inch loaf pan.

Cream the butter and sugar until light and fluffy. Add the eggs, one at a time, beating well after each addition. Stir in the cream.

Sift together the flour, baking powder, and cardamom. Add this and the lemon rind to the butter mixture, mixing until thoroughly combined.

Pour into the pan and bake for 45 minutes. Allow to cool for 10 minutes before removing from the pan.

Serving suggestion: Serve with a scoop of lemon sherbet and sliced berries.

Yield: 10 to 12 slices

Heat Scale: Mild

A Dessert Feast from the East

And still she slept in an azure-lidded sleep,
In blanched linen, smooth and lavendered,
While he from forth the closet brought a heap
Of candied apple, quince, and plum, and gourd,
With jellies smoother than the creamy curd,
And lucent syrops, tinct with cinnamon;
Manna and dates, in argosy transferred
From Fez; and spiced dainties, every one,
From silken Samarcand to cedared Lebanon.
John Keats, "The Eve of St. Agnes"

Bisteeya

This interesting dessert—and maybe it's an entrée, too—is from Rosemary Ann Ogilvie, who wrote about the back roads of Morocco in *Chile Pepper* magazine. "These savory pastries are traditionally eaten with the fingers as is all the food in Morocco," she noted. "The trick to working with filo pastry is to always keep the sheets covered with a damp cloth to keep it from drying out."

Filling:

1   teaspoon ground red New Mexican chile

2   tablespoons vegetable oil

1   teaspoon ground ginger

1   cup water

1   medium onion, grated

½   teaspoon saffron threads, crushed

1   cup chopped fresh parsley

¼   teaspoon turmeric

1   cup powdered sugar

1   teaspoon ground cinnamon

5   eggs, lightly boiled and sliced Salt and pepper to taste

Combine all the ingredients for the filling together in a bowl.

Almond Mixture:

8   ounces blanched almonds, finely ground

1   cup powdered sugar

1   tablespoon ground cinnamon

In a bowl, combine the almond mixture ingredients.

Pastry:

2	packages Greek filo pastry	Powdered sugar
8	ounces butter	Ground cinnamon

To assemble, in the center of a sheet of filo pastry, place ½ cup filling and top with a little of the almond mixture. Fold the pastry over toward the center to cover the filling. Top with another sheet of filo and tuck the edges under to obtain a 3- or 4-inch square.

Melt the butter in a pan and fry each pastry on both sides until crisp and brown. Sift powdered sugar and cinnamon on top and serve immediately.

Yield: 6 to 8 servings

Heat Scale: Mild

Pod Pourri, Part 8

According to the FoodTRENDS '94 survey of 500 restaurateurs and food service managers, the top three types of ethnic restaurants expected to have the greatest growth were Mexican (34 percent), Caribbean (33 percent), and Thai (25 percent). . . . As reported in *Food Arts* magazine, chiles stand tall at the Rosa Mexicana restaurant in New York City—eight feet tall, in fact, because they are painted steel sculptures representing plant spirit gods of the Otomi people of San Pablito in Puebla, Mexico. . . . According to one pundit, those hot and spicy retail shops springing up all over the country are "the culinary headshops of their time". . . .

Guava Duff

On her tour of the Bahamas, *Chile Pepper* food editor Nancy Gerlach collected many great recipes, including Guava Duff, which can be considered the national dessert of the Bahamas. "Everyone makes it," she wrote, "and everyone has their own recipe. The dessert probably has its origins with the English steamed puddings and traditionally was cooked in cotton pillowcases."

Butter Sauce:

¼   cup butter or margarine
¾   cup sugar

1   egg
    Brandy (optional)

Cream the butter and sugar. Add the egg and brandy and blend well.

Guava Duff:

¼   cup butter or margarine
1   cup sugar
3   eggs, beaten
2   cups guava pulp (guava put
    through a sieve or food mill)

½   teaspoon freshly grated nutmeg
½   teaspoon ground cinnamon
¼   teaspoon ground cloves
3   cups flour
2   teaspoons baking powder

Cream the butter with the sugar. Add the eggs, guava, and spices and beat until smooth.

Sift together the flour and baking powder and add to the butter mixture. The dough should be stiff.

Place the mixture in the greased top of a double boiler and cook over boiling water; or use a can with a tight-fitting cover and place the can in a pan of boiling water about two-thirds from the top of the can. Steam for 3 hours.

Slice and serve with the butter sauce.

Yield: 6 to 8 servings

Heat Scale: Mild

Tropical Fruit Crepes with Chocolate

Our passion for tropical fruits is a result of many trips to the Caribbean, Mexico, Central America, and Asia. Virtually any fruit that can be sliced can be used in this recipe, but here we're staying with some that are readily available.

3 cups assorted minced fruits, such as papaya, mango, kiwi fruit, red bananas, blood oranges, and melons	6 crepes or thin pancakes
2 tablespoons peach preserves	1½ cups prepared chocolate fudge sauce
2 tablespoons Triple Sec or Cointreau	Mint leaves and confectioners' sugar

Combine the fruit, preserves, and liqueur in a nonmetallic bowl and mix gently. Let stand, covered, for 1 hour to blend the flavors.

Spoon about ½ cup of the fruit mixture onto each of the crepes and roll up. Transfer the crepes to dessert plates and spoon the chocolate fudge sauce over it. Garnish with the mint leaves and sprinkle a little confectioners' sugar over the crepes.

Yield: 6 servings

Heat Scale: Mild

Note: This recipe requires advance preparation.

Mexican Chocolate and Piñon Wedding Cookies

Based after the famous Mexican wedding cakes, these cookies make a great snack—or a fancy dessert when topped with ice cream, frozen yogurt, or sorbet. Ibarra chocolate is flavored with cinnamon and sugar and is available at gourmet shops and Latin markets.

¾ cup firmly packed brown sugar

¾ cup butter, softened

3 ounces Ibarra chocolate, melted

1 teaspoon vanilla

2 cups all-purpose flour

1 cup finely chopped pine nuts or pecans

Confectioners' sugar

Heat the oven to 350 degrees. In a large bowl, combine the brown sugar and butter. With a mixer, beat at medium speed, scraping the bowl often, until the mixture is creamy, about 2 minutes.

Add the chocolate and vanilla and continue beating, about 2 more minutes. Reduce the mixer speed to low and add the flour and nuts. Continue beating, scraping the bowl, until well mixed, about 2 more minutes.

Shape the dough into balls with a 1-inch diameter and place 2 inches apart on cookie sheets. Bake for 8 to 10 minutes, then remove and let stand for 5 minutes. Carefully remove the cookies from the sheets and roll them in the confectioners' sugar. To serve as a dessert, place four cookies in a bowl and top with your favorite ice cream.

Yield: About 5 dozen cookies

Heat Scale: Mild

Hawaiian Vintage Chocolate Soufflé

This recipe is from Chef Philippe Padovani of Manele Bay Hotel on the Hawaiian island of Lana'i. It conjures up fond memories for Melissa, who first tasted Hawaiian Vintage Chocolate on her culinary tour of the islands. She observes: "Hawaiian Vintage Chocolate really will make you want to forsake any other chocolate forever. You may substitute your favorite chocolate if the Hawaiian Vintage is not available, but trust me, it won't be the same."

3	ounces Hawaiian Vintage Chocolate, melted, or use your favorite chocolate	8	egg whites
		4	tablespoons sugar
			Powdered sugar
4	teaspoons cognac		
4	egg yolks		

Preheat the oven to 375 degrees. Grease the sides of four small soufflé bowls and then coat each with sugar.

Combine the chocolate, cognac, and egg yolks in a bowl.

In a separate bowl, whip the egg whites with the sugar until peaks are formed. Using a spatula, fold the egg whites into the chocolate mixture and carefully mix.

Pour the mixture into the bowls and bake for 12 minutes or until the soufflé is firm.

Sprinkle with powdered sugar and serve immediately.

Yield: 4 servings

Heat Scale: Mild

Daiquiri Tarts

Made with the ingredients of the famous drink, these tangy tarts are quick and delicious. If you can find them, use the Key or Mexican limes in preference to the larger Persian limes.

½	cup fresh lime juice	2	tablespoons melted unsalted butter
1	tablespoon light rum	2	tablespoons confectioners' sugar
½	cup granulated sugar	½	cup whipped cream
2	large eggs, slightly beaten		
1	strip lime zest, 1 by 2 inches		
1	package frozen 3-inch pastry shells (not puff pastry)		

In the top of a double boiler, combine the lime juice, rum, sugar, eggs, and zest. Set the top over (not in) lightly boiling water and whisk the mixture constantly until thick enough to coat the back of a spoon, about 5 minutes. Strain the mixture into a bowl and allow to cool to room temperature, whisking occasionally.

Heat the oven to 400 degrees. Arrange the pastry shells on a baking sheet and bake until firm and lightly browned. Brush the shells with the melted butter and sprinkle the confectioners' sugar over them. Return the shells to the oven and bake for 3 to 5 minutes or until golden-brown.

Divide the lime mixture among the shells and top with a dollop of whipped cream.

Yield: 12 tarts

Heat Scale: Mild

Apple Crisp with Raisins and Vanilla Yogurt Topping

Use baking apples for this recipe—Granny Smith or Rome Beauty are preferred. You can serve the crisp with whipped cream, of course, but we've come up with a less caloric and fatty option.

¾ cup fresh whole wheat bread-crumbs

¼ cup firmly packed dark brown sugar

¾ teaspoon ground cinnamon

¼ teaspoon ground allspice

6 large baking apples (about 2½ pounds), peeled, cored, and sliced ½-inch thick

½ cup raisins

1 tablespoon freshly squeezed lemon juice

⅓ cup cider

2 tablespoons unsalted butter, chilled and cut into small pieces

1 cup vanilla yogurt

1 tablespoon honey

¼ teaspoon nutmeg

Preheat the oven to 375 degrees.

In a bowl, combine the breadcrumbs, sugar, cinnamon, and allspice. In another bowl, combine the apples and raisins and toss with the lemon juice.

Spray a 2½-quart baking dish with nonstick cooking spray. Place half the apple mixture in the dish and pour the cider over it. Dot with half the butter and sprinkle with half the breadcrumbs. Add the remaining apples, then top with the remaining butter and crumbs.

Bake, uncovered, until the crumbs are golden-brown, about 35 minutes.

In a bowl, combine the yogurt, honey, and nutmeg.

Serve the crisp warm, topped with the yogurt.

Yield: 6 servings

Heat Scale: Mild

Flan à la Antigua

This recipe is from Traci Des Jardins, executive chef of Rubicon in San Francisco. She featured it in *Chile Pepper*'s article "Jazz Up Your Holiday Season." Traci noted: "I come from a Mexican family, and we have always done a traditional Christmas Eve celebration at my parents' house, which is attended by my maternal grandmother, aunts, uncles, cousins, and friends. This is just the dessert to top off a perfect feast." This recipe requires advance preparation, and yes, it is a high-fat recipe, so beware!

2	cups milk	7	eggs
1	vanilla bean, split	1	teaspoon vanilla extract
1	(14-ounce) can condensed milk	1½	cups sugar

Preheat the oven to 350 degrees.

Heat the milk along with the vanilla bean, being careful not to let it boil. Add the condensed milk.

Whisk the eggs, vanilla, and ½ cup of the sugar together and gradually add the hot milk. Mix well and strain through a coarse strainer.

Moisten the remaining 1 cup of sugar with a little water and begin cooking over medium-high heat. Cook until the sugar is a deep brown color and gives off the fragrance of caramel. While still hot, pour into a 9-inch glass cake pan and coat the bottom and sides with the caramel. Pour the custard mixture over the caramel.

The custard must be baked in a *baña maria*, or water bath. To make a water bath, place the custard pan inside of a large roasting pan and then fill the roasting pan with hot tap water until it comes halfway up the side of the custard pan.

Bake the custard for 1 hour and 10 minutes, or until the center is just firm to the touch. Chill for 10 hours or more.

To serve, loosen the edges of the custard by running a knife around the perimeter. Place a platter over the custard and then invert the custard. Cut into wedges and spoon some of the caramel sauce over each serving.

Yield: 8 to 10 servings

Heat Scale: Mild

Relatively Low-Fat Hot Chocolate Pudding

We end the recipes in this book with a revamped return to our childhood. Here's the now culinary-correct version of a traditional favorite that's spiced up with two mild chile powers with hints of raisin. To make chile powders, remove the seeds and stems, dry the pods until brittle in the oven, then grind in a spice mill. As for the fat—about 3 grams per serving.

⅔	cup unsweetened cocoa powder	½	cup sugar
2	tablespoons cornstarch	⅛	teaspoon salt
½	teaspoon ancho chile powder	2	egg whites, slightly beaten
½	teaspoon pasilla chile powder	1	teaspoon vanilla extract
2½	cups skim milk		Fresh blackberries

In a bowl, combine the cocoa, cornstarch, ancho powder, and pasilla powder. Whisk ¼ cup of the milk into the mixture until smooth.

In a large saucepan, combine the remaining 2¼ cups of milk, sugar, and salt and stir well. Bring to a boil over high heat and continue boiling for 2 minutes. Remove the pan from the heat and whisk the cocoa mixture into the hot milk, stirring constantly. When mixed, return the pan to the heat and boil for 2 minutes.

Remove from the heat and add 1 cup of this mixture to the egg whites in a bowl, whisking well. Return this mixture to the pan and cook over medium heat for 2 minutes, taking care not to let it boil.

Remove the pan from the heat, add the vanilla, and mix well. Pour into individual custard dishes and chill in the refrigerator for at least 1½ hours.

Serve garnished with the blackberries.

Yield: 4 servings

Heat Scale: Mild

Note: This recipe requires advance preparation.

Red Hot Candy for Cancer Pain

In a beautifully ironic twist for a natural chemical falsely accused of causing stomach cancer, capsaicin has been shown to be "absolutely effective" in alleviating the pain from oral stomatitis, mouth sores caused by cancer chemotherapy and radiation treatments, according to Dr. Ann M. Berger of Yale University's Pain Management Center. The painful sores "can be overwhelming to the point that some people can't eat and have to stop treatment," Dr. Berger noted.

But capsaicin came to the rescue because of a unique partnership between Yale researchers Dr. Tracy Karrer, who showed conclusively that the fiery substance could eliminate oral pain, and Wolffe Nadoolman, a Wall Street stock analyst turned medical student, who had the idea to administer the capsaicin through a candy. The McCormick Spice Company of Hunt Valley, Maryland, donated the cayenne powder, and the metabolic kitchen at Yale's General Clinical Research Center cooked up the candies, which were butterscotch brittle. Patients at the Comprehensive Cancer Center donated their sore mouths, and the result was what the *Yale Alumni* magazine described as "a hot new treatment for a debilitating side effect of cancer treatment." Thanks to Will Amatruda, Colleen M. Karuza, and Robert G. Lee, M.D., for sending us information on this breakthrough.

A Pepper Primer

There are li̇t... ls of varieties of peppers grown in the world,
but onl... used for cooking in the United States and
... not intended to be exhaustive but is rather a
... pular peppers used in this country.

... the garden or market, fresh peppers are
... y become more commonly available. The
... rse, the familiar bells, which have no heat
... -Bell, which has a mild bite. The most
... brightly colored ones, which come in a
... nge to red to purple. They are most
... ads. The poblano, similar in size to a
... te to mild heat and is often stuffed

... s in the produce sections of super-
... pers. The yellow wax peppers are
... d for use in salsas and salads.
... ed in a similar manner; they are
... ovide a little extra bite and are
... ety that sometimes appears fresh is the
... pper is often pickled.

... eral varieties of the long, green New Mexican chiles avail-
... in the Southwest and occasionally other locations. The No. 6-4
variety is the most commonly grown and is available from August through
early November. It's hotter cousin, Sandia, is usually not seen in the green,
or immature, form. The mildest New Mexican variety is the Anaheim, a California variety that is available most of the year. Occasionally, New Mexican
chiles are identified by their grower (such as Barker) or by a regional appella-
tion (Chimayo or Hatch or Luna County), which further confuses the issue.

All of these long green chiles must be roasted and peeled before use in a
recipe. Blistering or roasting the chile is the process of heating the chile to the

point that the tough transparent skin is separated from the meat of the chile so it can be removed. The method is quite simple.

While processing the chiles, be sure to wear rubber gloves to protect yourself from the capsaicin that can burn your hands and any other part of your body that you touch. Before roasting, cut a small slit in the chiles close to the top so that the steam can escape. The chiles can then be placed on a baking sheet and put directly under the broiler or on a screen on the top of the stove.

Our favorite method (which involves meditation and a bottle of Negro Modelo) is to place the pods on a charcoal grill about five to six inches from the coals. Blisters will soon indicate that the skin is separating, but be sure that the chiles are blistered all over or they will not peel properly. Immediately wrap the chiles in damp towels or place in a plastic bag for ten to fifteen minutes—this "steams" them and loosens the skins. For crisper, less-cooked chile, plunge them into ice water to stop the cooking process.

Green chile is a low-acid fruit, and for that reason we do not recommend the home canning of it. It can be done, but only by using a pressure canner and by carefully following all the manufacturer's specific instructions. We find freezing to be a much easier and more flavorful method of preservation.

If they are to be frozen whole (rather than chopped), the pods do not have to be peeled first. In fact, they are easier to peel after they have been frozen. After roasting the chiles, freeze them in the form that you plan to use them—whole, in strips, or chopped. If you are storing in strips or chopped, peel the pods first. A handy way to put up chopped or diced chiles is to freeze them in ice cube trays with sections. When frozen, they can be "popped" out of the trays and stored in a bag in the freezer. When making a soup or a stew, just drop in a cube! This eliminates the problems inherent in hacking apart a large slab of frozen chiles when you just need a couple of ounces.

New Mexican chiles are available fresh in season by overnight delivery (see Appendix 2, "Mail-Order Sources"). They are found canned in most U.S. markets and frozen in some parts of the Southwest.

Other fresh chiles that are sometimes found in markets (especially farmers' markets) are serranos and habaneros. The serranos—smaller, thinner, and hotter than jalapeños—are the classic chiles of the Mexican *pico de gallo* fresh salsas. Habaneros, the world's hottest peppers, are lantern-shaped orange or red devils that have a unique, fruity aroma in addition to their powerful punch. Use them with caution. Generally speaking, any of the small fresh peppers may be substituted for each other; however, they are not a substitute for poblanos or the New Mexican varieties in recipes. The smaller chiles—habaneros, serranos, and jalapeños—can be frozen without processing. Wash the chiles, dry them, and put them one layer deep on a cookie sheet and freeze. After they are frozen solid, store them in a bag. Frozen chiles will keep for nine months to a year at 0 degrees F. All of the small peppers can be frozen whole with no further processing needed, and their texture holds up surprisingly well in the freezer.

Dried Peppers. As is true with fresh peppers, the larger they are, the milder. The large dried peppers, such as ancho (a dried poblano) and the New Mexican varieties, are mild enough to be the principal ingredients of sauces. The smaller varieties, such as piquin, are too hot for this purpose and are generally used as condiments or in stir-frying. All dried peppers can be ground into powders (see below).

There are four main large peppers used as the base for sauces: ancho, pasilla, New Mexican, and guajillo. The ancho is a wide, dark pepper with a raisiny aroma. It is the only pepper that is commonly stuffed in its dried form (the pod is softened in water first). The pasilla is a long, thin, dark pepper that also has a raisiny or a nutty aroma. Along with the ancho, it commonly appears in Mexican *mole* sauces.

The most common use of the red New Mexican chiles is to hang them in long strings, or *ristras*, until they are ready to be used in cooking. Then, they are commonly rehydrated and combined with onions, garlic, oil, spices, and water to make the classic New Mexican red chile sauce, a common topping for enchiladas in the Southwest. The guajillos, a shortened and hotter version of the New Mexican chiles, are commonly used in sauces in northern Mexico.

Another favorite dried chile pepper is the chipotle, a smoke-dried red jalapeño that has a fiery, smoky flavor. It is available loose in the dried form or canned in adobo sauce. The latter is easier to use, because it's already rehydrated. To rehydrate the dried chipotles, simply soak them in hot water for an hour or more.

There are a bewildering number of small, hot pods ranging in size from that of a little fingernail (the chiltepin) to the six-inch, skinny cayenne. Some varieties include piquin, Thai, santaka, de arbol, mirasol, and tabasco. These chiles appear in stir-fry dishes, are floated in soups or stews, or are used to add heat to sauces that are too mild.

Powders. All chiles can be dried and ground into powder—and most are, including the habanero. Crushed chiles, or those coarsely ground with some of the seeds, are called *quebrado*. Coarse powders are referred to as *caribe*, while the finer powders are termed *molido*. The milder powders, such as New Mexican, can also be used as the base for sauces, but the hotter powders, such as cayenne and piquin, are used when heat is needed more than flavor. In our homes, we actually have more powders available than whole pods, because the powders are concentrated and take up less storage space. We store them in small, airtight bottles. The fresher the powders, the better they taste, so don't grind up too many pods. Use an electric spice mill and be sure to wear a painter's mask to protect the nose and throat from the pungent powder. The colors of the powders vary from a bright, electric red-orange (chiltepins) to light green (dried jalapeños) to a dark brown that verges on black (ancho). We love to experiment by changing the powders called for in recipes.

Other Chile Products. A vast number of foods and condiments now contain chile peppers. Quite a few of these products are handy for cooks who love all things hot and spicy and meatless. Look for chile-infused vinegars, oils, mustards, ketchup, cheeses, pickles, hot sauces, salad dressings, jams and jellies, soups, pastas, potato and corn chips, curry powders and pastes, nuts, and even candies.

Mail-Order Sources

Hundreds of companies carry chile pepper products; it's impossible to list them all here. The companies below carry a wide variety of ingredients and products mentioned in the recipes in this book. Another great resource for more companies and recipes is *Chile Pepper* magazine.

Chile Pepper Magazine
1227 West Magnolia
Garden Level Suite
Fort Worth, TX 76104
(888) SPICY HOT (774-2946)

Caribbean Food Products
1936 N. Second Avenue
Jacksonville Beach, FL 32250
(904) 246-0149
Mail-order source for Trinidadian Congo pepper sauces.

Chile Today, Hot Tamale
919 Highway 33, Ste. 47
Freehold, NJ 07728
(800) 468-7377
Mail-order source for habanero hot sauces and other products.

Coyote Cocina
1364 Rufina Circle #1
Santa Fe, NM 87501
(800) 866-HOWL (866-4695)
Mail-order source for hot sauces and other chile products.

Dat'l Do It
P.O. Box 4019
St. Augustine, FL 32084
(800) HOT-DATL (468-3285)
Grower of fresh Datil peppers; manufacturer of Datil pepper products, Datil pepper seeds.

Dean and DeLuca
Mail-Order Department
560 Broadway
New York, NY 10012
(212) 431-1691
Exotic herbs and spices from around the world.

Don Alfonso Foods
P.O. Box 201988
Austin, TX 78720
(800) 456-6100
Imported Mexican chiles; chipotles in adobo in glass containers.

Enchanted Seeds
P.O. Box 6087
Las Cruces, NM 88006
(505) 233-3033
Habanero and other exotic chile seeds.

Frieda's, Inc.
P.O. Box 584888
Los Angeles, CA 90058
(800) 421-9477
*Shipper of fresh and dried habaneros,
other chiles, and exotic produce.*

Gil's Gourmet Gallery
577 Ortiz Avenue
Sand City, CA 93955
(800) 438-7480
*Mail-order source for habanero hot
sauces and other products.*

Hot Sauce Harry's
The Dallas Farmer's Market
3422 Flair Drive
Dallas, TX 75229
(214) 902-8552
A large collection of hot sauces.

Le Saucier
Faneuil Hall Marketplace
Boston, MA 02109
(617) 227-9649
*Sauces, sauces, and condiments from all
over the world.*

Melissa's World Variety Produce
P.O. Box 21127
Los Angeles, CA 90021
(800) 468-7111
*Shipper of fresh, dried, and pickled chiles
and other specialty produce.*

Mo Hotta, Mo Betta
P.O. Box 4136
San Luis Obispo, CA 93403
(800) 462-3220
A wide collection of chile products.

Old Southwest Trading Company
P.O. Box 7545
Albuquerque, NM 87194
(505) 836-0168
*New Mexican and Mexican chiles;
sauces and salsas, Southwest gifts.*

Pendery's
1221 Manufacturing
Dallas, TX 75207
(800) 533-1870
*Dried chiles, spices, and other chile
products.*

Santa Fe School of Cooking
116 W. San Francisco Street
Santa Fe, NM 87501
(505) 983-4511
*Mail-order source for chile seeds, dried
and pickled pods, and other hot and
spicy products.*

Shepherd's Garden Seeds
6116 Highway 9
Felton, CA 95108
(408) 335-5216
Chile pepper and exotic vegetable seeds.

Stonewall Chile Pepper Company
P.O. Box 241
Stonewall, TX 78671
(800) 232-2995
*Habanero products, including salsas
and ketchup.*

Bibliography

Chalmers, Irene. *The Great Food Almanac.* San Francisco: CollinsPublishers, 1994.

Chávez, Denise. "Scenes of Home and a Green Dream." *New Mexico Magazine*, March, 1996, 32.

Chotzinoff, Robin. *People with Dirty Hands: The Passion for Gardening.* New York: Macmillan Reference, 1996.

DeWitt, Dave and Mary Jane Wilan and Melissa T. Stock. *Hot & Spicy & Meatless.* Rocklin, CA: Prima Publishing, 1994.

Elkhort, Martin. *The Secret Life of Food.* Los Angeles: Jeremy P. Tarcher, 1991.

Fisher, M. F. K. *The Art of Eating.* New York: Collier Books, 1990.

Fitzgibbon, Theodora. *The Pleasures of the Table.* Oxford: Oxford University Press, 1981.

Leckie, Ross. *The Gourmet's Companion.* Edinburgh, Scotland: Edinburgh Publishing Co., 1993.

Mackay, Ian. *Food for Thought.* Freedom, CA: The Crossing Press, 1995.

Mares, E. A. "Tony." "Duende and the Divine Comedy." *New Mexico Magazine*, March, 1996, 38.

Robbins, Maria Polushkin. *The Cook's Quotation Book.* New York: Penguin, 1984.

Robbins, Maria Polushkin. *A Cook's Alphabet of Quotations.* New York: Dutton Books, 1991.

Root, Waverly and Richard de Rochemont. *Eating in America.* Hopewell, N.J.: The Ecco Press, 1981.

Sagel, Jim. "Chile del Norte." *New Mexico Magazine*, March, 1996, 26.

Smith, Andrew F. *The Tomato in America.* Columbia, S.C.: University of South Carolina Press, 1994.

Trager, James. *The Food Chronology.* New York: Henry Holt & Co., 1995.

Voorhees, Don. *Why Does Popcorn Pop?* New York: Citadel Press, 1995.

Weil, Dr. Andrew. "Eating Chiles." In *The Marriage of the Sun and Moon.* New York: Houghton-Mifflin Co., 1980.

Index